The Ultimate Sourdough Starter Bible for Busy Families

Foolproof Recipes, Zero Waste Hacks, and Step-by-Step Bread Baking for Delicious, Homemade Family Meals Without Breaking The Bank

TABLE OF CONTENTS

SCAN THE QR CODE OR SELECT THE LINK TO **ACCESS AND DOWNLOAD THE BONUS.**

https://drive.google.com/file/d/1y5SANl7vyhQcal5zgezktSvXcuMRJ1ZC/view?usp=sharing

INTRODUCTION:WHY EVERY FAMILY NEEDS SOURDOUGH IN THEIR KITCHEN

Sourdough is more than bread—it's a time-honored tradition linking generations of bakers. While it may seem complex in today's fast-paced world, mastering sourdough doesn't require expensive tools or excessive time. This book simplifies the process, offering essential techniques to create bakery-quality bread and flavorful meals with ease. Say goodbye to stress and waste—embrace the art of sourdough and elevate your home baking experience.

How this book will transform your baking—zero waste, maximum flavor, and stress-free methods

This book redefines sourdough baking, making it accessible and stress-free. Traditional methods can feel overwhelming, but this guide simplifies the process into easy, flexible steps that fit any schedule. A key focus is eliminating waste—rather than discarding sourdough starter, you'll learn how to transform it into delicious snacks, meals, and desserts like pretzels, pancakes, and pizza crust. Beyond waste reduction, the book emphasizes maximizing flavor through natural fermentation, offering insights on how timing and temperature influence taste. With clear explanations, practical tips, and adaptable techniques, you'll gain the confidence to create customized loaves without rigid schedules or complex methods. Whether you're a beginner or an experienced baker, this book provides a fresh approach that enhances flavor, minimizes waste, and makes sourdough baking an enjoyable, rewarding experience.

The Busy Family Baking Method: Sourdough without the long, complicated process

The **Busy Family Baking Method** revolutionizes traditional sourdough baking, making it accessible, efficient, and adaptable to modern, busy lifestyles. Unlike conventional methods that demand constant attention and rigid timing, this approach allows bakers to fit sourdough into their schedules with flexible, manageable steps. Dough preparation can be broken down over a day or multiple days, utilizing techniques like **stretch-and-fold** instead of labor-intensive kneading. Overnight fermentation enhances flavor while requiring minimal effort. The method also prioritizes **simplicity**, using common kitchen tools instead of specialized equipment, with budget-friendly alternatives for those looking to expand their setup. By eliminating unnecessary complexity, this book empowers anyone—regardless of experience—to enjoy **homemade, bakery-quality sourdough** without stress. Whether juggling work, family, or other responsibilities, bakers can now create **nutritious, delicious bread** with ease, proving that great sourdough doesn't require an all-day commitment.

CHAPTER 1: THE FOOLPROOF SOURDOUGH STARTER – NO MORE FAILURES!

Every great sourdough begins with a starter—a living culture of flour and water that gives your bread its rise, flavor, and character. But for many beginners, creating a starter can feel like the most intimidating part of the process. It doesn't have to be. This chapter takes the mystery out of sourdough starters, guiding you step by step to create a healthy, active culture that never fails. Whether you're a first-time baker or have struggled before, you'll learn foolproof methods that make starting and maintaining your sourdough simple and stress-free.

What is a sourdough starter, and why is it essential?

A sourdough starter is the foundation of every sourdough loaf, a living culture of flour and water that captures wild yeast and beneficial bacteria. Unlike commercial yeast, it fosters a natural fermentation process, enhancing flavor, texture, and nutritional value. The interplay of wild yeast and lactic acid bacteria creates the signature tangy taste and airy crumb, while slow fermentation strengthens gluten structure for a superior bite. Additionally, it improves digestibility by breaking down phytic acid and pre-digesting gluten. A well-maintained starter can last indefinitely, deepening in complexity over time, and is often passed down through generations. More than an ingredient, it is a living element of baking that allows for customization and mastery. Understanding its role unlocks the potential for crafting exceptional, bakery-quality bread at home.

Step-by-step guide: How to create your first starter

Creating your first sourdough starter might seem daunting, but it's simpler than you think. With just two basic ingredients—flour and water—you can cultivate a living culture that will become the foundation of all your sourdough baking. This guide walks you through each step, ensuring success even if you've never worked with sourdough before. The process takes about five to seven days, and while it requires a little patience, the result is a robust, bubbly starter that will reward you with flavorful, bakery-quality bread for years to come.

What You'll Need:

- **Flour:** Start with unbleached all-purpose flour or whole wheat flour. Whole wheat contains more natural yeast and bacteria, which helps the starter get going faster.
- **Water:** Use filtered or bottled water at room temperature. Tap water can contain chlorine, which may interfere with fermentation.
- **A clear glass jar or container:** This allows you to observe the activity and growth. Make sure it's large enough to hold the expanding starter.
- **A spoon or spatula:** For mixing. Avoid metal utensils, as they can react with the starter's acidity.
- **A loose lid or cloth cover:** The starter needs to breathe, so don't use an airtight lid. A paper towel or cheesecloth secured with a rubber band works well.

Day 1: Getting Started

- **Combine ½ cup (60 grams) of flour** and **¼ cup (60 ml) of water** in your jar. Mix until all the flour is hydrated, and you have a thick, sticky dough.
- **Scrape down the sides** of the jar, cover loosely, and leave it at room temperature (70-75°F is ideal). This begins the fermentation process, allowing wild yeast and bacteria to colonize the mixture.
- **What to expect:** Not much will happen today. The mixture will look like a thick paste. This is normal—no need to worry.

Day 2: Checking for Signs of Life

- **Stir the mixture** to distribute any developing yeast. You may notice small bubbles forming, a sign that fermentation is beginning. The smell might be slightly sweet or fruity, which is a good indication that wild yeast is growing.
- **Add another ½ cup of flour and ¼ cup of water.** Mix thoroughly, scrape down the sides, and cover loosely again.
- **What to expect:** You should see more bubbles, and the mixture may rise slightly before falling back. The smell might become more tangy or sour.

Days 3 to 5: Establishing the Culture

- **Feed the starter once a day:** Discard half of the mixture (about ½ cup) to avoid overwhelming the growing yeast. Then add **½ cup of flour and ¼ cup of water**. Mix well, scrape down the sides, and cover loosely.
- **Watch for activity:** By Day 3, your starter should be visibly bubbly and rise after feeding, sometimes doubling in size within 4 to 6 hours. This shows that the wild yeast is thriving.
- **Smell and texture check:** The aroma should become more sour, like yogurt or vinegar. The texture will be airy and spongy. If the smell is off-putting or if you see mold, discard the starter and start over.

Day 6: Building Strength and Consistency

- **Increase feeding frequency:** Feed the starter every 12 hours (morning and evening). Continue to discard half and add fresh flour and water each time. This boosts the yeast population and stabilizes the culture.
- **Check for readiness:** The starter is ready when it consistently doubles in size within 4 to 6 hours of feeding and has a pleasant, tangy aroma. It should be bubbly and elastic, with a slightly spongy texture.

Day 7: The Float Test

- To confirm that your starter is active and ready to bake, perform the **float test.** Drop a spoonful of starter into a glass of water. If it **floats**, it's ready to use. If it **sinks**, continue feeding for another day or two until it passes the test.

Ongoing Maintenance and Storage

- **Daily feeding:** If you bake frequently, keep the starter at room temperature and feed it once daily.
- **Refrigeration:** If you bake less often, store the starter in the fridge and feed it once a week. Before baking, bring it back to room temperature and feed it twice to reactivate.

Tips for Success:

- **Consistency is key:** Try to feed the starter at the same time each day to establish a rhythm.
- **Adjusting hydration:** If the starter is too thick, add a little more water. If it's too runny, add a little more flour. The consistency should be like thick pancake batter.
- **Troubleshooting:** If the starter stops bubbling or develops a pink or orange tint, it's contaminated. Discard and start fresh.

By following this step-by-step guide, you'll create a strong, active sourdough starter that becomes your trusted kitchen companion. This living culture is the foundation for all your sourdough baking, giving you the power to create delicious, nutritious bread with depth of flavor that's unmatched by commercial yeast. With patience and care, your starter will grow more robust over time, becoming an heirloom of flavor to pass down through generations.

The 3-Day vs. 7-Day Starter: Which method works best for you?

Choosing the right method to create your sourdough starter depends on your schedule, patience level, and baking goals. Both the 3-day and 7-day methods can yield a strong, active starter, but they have different advantages and challenges. Understanding the differences will help you decide which approach fits your lifestyle.

The 3-Day Starter Method

The 3-day method is ideal for those who want quick results and are eager to start baking. It uses a higher ratio of whole wheat flour, which is rich in natural yeast and bacteria, speeding up the fermentation process. This method requires more frequent feedings and a warm environment (ideally 75-80°F) to encourage rapid yeast growth. By the end of the third day, the starter should be bubbly, active, and ready to use.

Pros:

- **Speed:** You can start baking in as little as three days, making this method perfect for those with limited time.
- **Intense Flavor:** Rapid fermentation creates a bold, tangy flavor that sourdough lovers appreciate.
- **Minimal Waste:** Shorter feeding duration means less discard, making it a more waste-conscious option.

Cons:

- **Less Stability:** Rapid fermentation can produce inconsistent results. The starter may need more time to fully mature and stabilize.
- **High Maintenance:** Requires frequent feeding (every 8-12 hours) and close monitoring of temperature and activity.
- **Shorter Lifespan:** Starters made quickly may not have the long-term resilience of those developed more slowly.

The 7-Day Starter Method

The 7-day method takes a slower, more gradual approach, allowing the wild yeast and bacteria to fully develop and stabilize. It uses a balanced mix of all-purpose and whole wheat flours, producing a milder, more versatile starter. This method is more forgiving, requiring less frequent feedings (once every 24 hours) and adapting well to room temperature conditions.

Pros:

- **Greater Stability:** A slower fermentation process creates a more balanced ecosystem of yeast and bacteria, leading to consistent, reliable results.
- **Milder Flavor:** This method produces a more subtle, nuanced sourness that works well in a variety of recipes, from bread to pastries.
- **Lower Maintenance:** Feeding once a day is less demanding, making this method ideal for busy schedules or first-time bakers.

Cons:

- **Takes Longer:** The extended timeline requires more patience, which may not suit those eager to bake immediately.
- **More Discard:** A longer feeding cycle generates more discard, although this can be minimized by using the recipes provided in this book.
- **Less Tangy:** The flavor is milder compared to the 3-day method, which may not satisfy those craving a bold sourdough taste.

Which Method is Right for You?

If you're short on time, want a bold, tangy flavor, and are comfortable with a more hands-on approach, the **3-day method** is a great choice. It's perfect for adventurous bakers who don't mind experimenting and adjusting as they go. However, if you prefer a more laid-back process with consistent, reliable results, the **7-day method** is the better option. It's especially suitable for beginners, busy families, or those who want a versatile starter that can be used in a wide range of recipes.

Whichever method you choose, the key is to be patient and flexible. Sourdough starters are living cultures, influenced by variables like temperature, flour type, and even the environment in your kitchen. If one method doesn't work perfectly the first time, don't get discouraged. Simply adjust the feeding schedule, temperature, or flour blend and try again. With a little practice, you'll find the approach that works best for you, ensuring a strong, reliable starter that brings delicious, bakery-quality sourdough to your kitchen.

Chapter 2: Mastering the Basics – Simple Techniques for Artisan Bread Success

Mastering sourdough isn't about complicated techniques or expensive tools—it's about understanding the basics. In this chapter, you'll learn the fundamental skills needed to create artisan bread with a beautiful crust, open crumb, and rich flavor. By focusing on simple, effective methods, you'll gain the confidence to bake like a pro, even if you're just starting out. From balancing hydration levels to perfecting fermentation and learning the easiest way to handle dough, these techniques are designed to fit seamlessly into your busy life, giving you consistently delicious results every time.

Understanding hydration levels and how they affect your bread

Hydration is a crucial factor in sourdough baking, determining texture, crust, crumb structure, and fermentation. Expressed as a percentage, hydration is the ratio of water to flour in the dough. Higher hydration (75%-85%) yields an open, airy crumb with large holes and a thin, crisp crust but requires advanced handling techniques due to stickiness. Moderate hydration (65%-70%) balances ease of shaping with a soft, tender crumb, making it ideal for beginners. Lower hydration (60%-65%) results in firmer dough, a tighter crumb, and a thicker crust, suitable for sandwich bread and rolls. Hydration also influences fermentation speed—higher hydration accelerates enzyme and yeast activity, enhancing flavor complexity but requiring close monitoring to prevent over-fermentation. Additionally, temperature and flour type affect hydration; warmer conditions increase elasticity, while different flours absorb water differently. Mastering hydration involves balancing dough consistency, fermentation, and handling techniques. Beginners should start with lower hydration and gradually increase as they gain confidence. Instead of adding flour to combat stickiness, techniques like stretch-and-fold or resting periods can improve dough manageability. Understanding and adjusting hydration levels allows bakers to refine texture, flavor, and structure, ultimately achieving the desired sourdough characteristics.

The secret to perfect fermentation: How to know when your dough is ready

Fermentation is the core process in sourdough baking, responsible for the bread's rise, flavor, and texture. During fermentation, wild yeast and bacteria in the starter consume flour sugars, producing gases that expand the dough and acids that enhance taste and freshness. Achieving the right fermentation balance is crucial for optimal bread quality. Key indicators of proper fermentation include volume, texture, and elasticity. The dough should expand 1.5 to 2 times its original size—under-proofed dough remains dense, while over-proofed dough may collapse. Texture is another essential factor; properly fermented dough feels airy and springy. The "poke test" helps assess readiness: if an indentation slowly springs back but leaves a slight dent, the dough is proofed correctly. Immediate rebound signals under-proofing, while a deep, unresponsive dent indicates over-proofing. Temperature significantly affects fermentation speed—warmer conditions (75-85°F) accelerate the process, while cooler ones (65-70°F) slow it down. Adjusting the environment helps maintain control. Aroma is another useful gauge: well-fermented dough has a mild, sweet-sour scent, whereas an overly sour or alcohol-like smell suggests over-fermentation. Mastering fermentation requires practice and keen observation rather than reliance on timers. By monitoring volume, texture, elasticity, and aroma, bakers can develop intuition for perfect fermentation, ensuring consistently high-quality sourdough.

Stretch & fold vs. kneading—what's easiest for busy bakers?

Working with sourdough dough can be intimidating, especially when it comes to gluten development. Traditional kneading, while effective, is labor-intensive, requiring 10 to 15 minutes of active work on a floured surface to align gluten strands and create the bread's structure. However, the stretch and fold method offers a simpler, less time-consuming alternative that achieves the same results with minimal effort. Instead of continuous kneading, this technique involves gently stretching and folding the dough at intervals during bulk fermentation—typically every 30 to 45 minutes, for a total of three to four rounds. Each session lasts just 30 seconds, allowing bakers to integrate the process into their daily routine effortlessly. This method is particularly beneficial for beginners and those working with high-hydration doughs, as it prevents overworking, reduces mess, and preserves the dough's elasticity. Unlike traditional kneading, stretch and fold is more forgiving, helping to create the airy crumb and chewy texture that define great sourdough. For busy bakers, this technique is a game-changer, making homemade sourdough more accessible without sacrificing quality.

Chapter 3 : Baking the Perfect Artisan Loaf – Without a Bakery Oven!

You don't need a commercial oven to bake beautiful artisan sourdough. With the right techniques and tools, you can achieve a crispy crust, open crumb, and rich flavor right in your home kitchen. This chapter shows you how to make the most of your everyday oven, using simple methods that deliver professional results. From choosing the best bakeware to mastering steam and heat distribution, you'll learn the secrets to creating bakery-quality sourdough without the fancy equipment. Get ready to impress your family with delicious, golden-brown loaves fresh from your own oven.

How to bake quality sourdough in your home oven

Baking high-quality sourdough at home is achievable with any oven by mastering heat distribution, steam, and timing. Conventional ovens, the most common, have uneven heat, requiring thorough preheating (at least 45 minutes) and a high temperature (475°F/246°C) for optimal oven spring. Using a pizza stone or baking steel helps stabilize heat. Convection ovens, equipped with a fan for even heat, bake faster; reducing the temperature by 25°F (14°C) prevents over-browning. Countertop toaster ovens can also work but need careful monitoring due to limited space; rotating the loaf ensures even browning. Steam is essential for crust development and expansion. A Dutch oven traps moisture for a steamy environment, while a steam tray offers an alternative for conventional ovens. Timing is crucial—start with 20 minutes of steam baking, then uncover for 20-25 minutes until golden brown. For an extra crisp crust, leave the bread in the turned-off oven with the door slightly open for 5-10 minutes. Understanding your oven's characteristics and making small adjustments will allow you to consistently bake artisan-quality sourdough at home.

The right tools (and budget-friendly alternatives)

Equipping yourself with the right tools simplifies sourdough baking, but achieving great results doesn't require expensive equipment. Many professional tools have affordable alternatives that work just as well. Understanding which tools are essential and which can be substituted helps you set up a functional sourdough kitchen on a budget. A **digital kitchen scale** is the most crucial tool, ensuring precise measurements for hydration and ingredient ratios. Affordable models are widely available, while measuring cups and spoons can work in a pinch with careful leveling. To mix and maintain a **starter**, a large, clear jar with a loose-fitting lid—such as a repurposed mason or pickle jar—is ideal, allowing for airflow and easy monitoring of activity. For **baking**, a **Dutch oven** creates the necessary steam for a crispy crust and excellent oven spring, but a heavy-duty stockpot, oven-safe casserole dish, or a preheated baking stone with a steam tray can serve as alternatives. A **bench scraper** aids in handling sticky dough, dividing portions, and cleaning surfaces. If unavailable, a flat spatula or even a sturdy credit card can substitute. **Proofing baskets (bannetons)** support dough during rising, but a flour-dusted towel inside a mixing bowl, colander, or wicker basket works as a budget-friendly replacement. For **scoring**, a **bread lame** ensures clean expansion cuts, but a sharp kitchen knife or a mounted razor blade works just as well. Finally, a **cooling rack** prevents soggy bottoms; an oven rack or propping the loaf on its side can achieve the same effect. With these essential tools and their affordable substitutes, you can bake high-quality sourdough bread without unnecessary expenses, proving that skill and technique matter more than costly equipment.

Secrets to crispy crust & soft crumb – professional techniques simplified

Achieving the ideal balance between a crispy crust and a soft, airy crumb defines exceptional sourdough. The secret lies in mastering steam, heat control, hydration, and fermentation. Steam during the first 15–20 minutes allows the dough to expand before the crust sets, while gelatinized starches create a crackly exterior. A preheated Dutch oven or a hot metal tray with boiling water ensures proper steam trapping. High heat—preheating the oven to 475°F (246°C) and lowering it to 450°F (232°C) after 20 minutes—promotes rapid expansion and even browning. Hydration (70–80%) and proper fermentation develop a tender crumb with complex flavors, while stretch-and-fold techniques build gluten strength. Cooling the bread completely prevents a gummy texture. By following these professional techniques, you can consistently bake sourdough with a golden crust and a light, flavorful interior.

NOW THAT YOU KNOW THE AUTHENTIC AND EFFECTIVE SECRETS TO START THIS EXTRAORDINARY ADVENTURE, IT'S TIME TO TAKE ACTION WITH THE BEST RECIPES. ARE YOU READY?
LET'S GET STARTED!

APPLE CINNAMON SOURDOUGH PANCAKES

Preparation time: 10 minutes
Cooking time: 15 minutes
Servings: 4 people

The picture is only demonstrative of the recipe.

Ingredients:

- 1 cup (9 oz/240 g) sourdough starter discard (unfed)
- 1 cup (4 oz/120 g) all-purpose flour
- 1 tablespoon (0,50 oz/12 g) sugar
- 1 teaspoon (0,15 oz/ 4 g) baking powder
- ½ teaspoon (0,11 oz/ 3 g) baking soda
- ½ teaspoon (0,7 oz/2 g) salt
- 1 teaspoon (0,11 oz/3 g) ground cinnamon
- 1 cup (240 ml) whole milk
- 1 large egg
- 2 tablespoons (0,11oz/30 g) unsalted butter, melted
- 1 medium apple, peeled, cored, and finely diced
- Butter or oil for cooking

Instructions:

1. **Combine dry ingredients:** In a large bowl, whisk together flour, sugar, baking powder, baking soda, salt, and cinnamon.
2. **Mix wet ingredients:** In another bowl, combine the sourdough starter, milk, egg, and melted butter. Whisk until smooth.
3. **Combine wet and dry:** Pour the wet mixture into the dry ingredients. Mix gently until just combined. Fold in the diced apples. The batter should be slightly lumpy—do not overmix.
4. **Preheat and cook:** Heat a non-stick skillet or griddle over medium heat (about 350°F / 175°C). Lightly grease with butter or oil. Pour ¼ cup of batter for each pancake onto the skillet.

5. **Flip and finish:** Cook until bubbles form on the surface and the edges look set (about 2-3 minutes). Flip and cook for another 2 minutes until golden brown and cooked through.
6. **Serve:** Serve hot with your favorite toppings, such as maple syrup, whipped cream, or additional apple slices.

Nutritional Values (per serving): Calories: 280 | Fat: 9g | Carbs: 42g | Protein: 6g | Fiber: 2g | Sugar: 10g | Sodium: 540mg

BANANA NUT SOURDOUGH MUFFINS

Preparation Time: 15 minutes
Cooking Time: 20 minutes
Servings: 4 people (Makes about 8 muffins)

The picture is only demonstrative of the recipe.

Ingredients:

- 1 cup (8,50 oz/240 g) ripe bananas, mashed (about 2 medium bananas)
- ½ cup (120 ml) sourdough discard (unfed)
- 1 large egg
- ¼ cup (60 ml) vegetable oil or melted coconut oil
- ⅓ cup (2,30 oz/65 g) brown sugar, packed
- 1 teaspoon vanilla extract
- 1 cup (4,50 oz/125 g) all-purpose flour
- ½ teaspoon baking soda
- ½ teaspoon baking powder
- ½ teaspoon ground cinnamon
- ¼ teaspoon salt
- ½ cup (2,15 oz/60 g) chopped walnuts or pecans

Instructions:

1. **Preheat the oven** to 375°F (190°C). Line a muffin tin with paper liners or grease well.
2. In a large bowl, **mix the mashed bananas, sourdough discard, egg, oil, brown sugar, and vanilla extract** until smooth and well combined.
3. In a separate bowl, **whisk together the flour, baking soda, baking powder, cinnamon, and salt.**
4. **Gradually add the dry ingredients** to the wet mixture, stirring gently until just combined. Do not overmix.
5. **Fold in the chopped nuts** using a spatula, ensuring they are evenly distributed throughout the batter.
6. **Spoon the batter** into the prepared muffin tin, filling each cup about ¾ full.
7. **Bake for 18-20 minutes** or until a toothpick inserted into the center comes out clean.
8. **Cool in the pan for 5 minutes,** then transfer to a wire rack to cool completely.

Nutritional Values (Per Muffin): Calories: 210 | Fat: 10g | Carbs: 28g | Fiber: 2g | Sugars: 14g | Protein: 4g

BLUEBERRY LEMON SOURDOUGH WAFFLES

Preparation Time: 10 minutes
Cooking Time: 15 minutes
Servings: 4 people

The picture is only demonstrative of the recipe.

Ingredients:

- 1 cup (8,50 oz/240 g) sourdough starter discard (unfed)
- 1 cup (240 ml) whole milk
- 2 large eggs
- ¼ cup (2,15 oz/60 g) melted unsalted butter
- 2 tablespoons (1,00 oz/30 g) granulated sugar
- 1 teaspoon (5 ml) vanilla extract
- 1½ cups (6,40 oz/180 g) all-purpose flour
- 1 tablespoon (15 g) baking powder
- ¼ teaspoon (0,60 oz/1.5 g) salt
- 1 cup (5,30 oz/150 g) fresh blueberries (or frozen, thawed and drained)
- Zest of one lemon

Instructions:

1. **Preheat your waffle iron** according to the manufacturer's instructions. For best results, set it to medium-high heat (around 375°F / 190°C).
2. **In a large bowl**, whisk together the sourdough starter discard, milk, eggs, melted butter, sugar, and vanilla extract until smooth and well combined.
3. **In a separate bowl**, mix the flour, baking powder, and salt. Gradually add the dry ingredients to the wet mixture, stirring until just combined. Be careful not to overmix.
4. **Fold in the blueberries and lemon zest** gently to avoid bursting the berries.
5. **Lightly grease the waffle iron** with non-stick spray or a small amount of melted butter. Pour the batter into the preheated waffle iron, spreading it evenly.
6. **Close the waffle iron** and cook for 3–5 minutes or until golden brown and crispy. The cooking time may vary depending on your waffle iron.
7. **Carefully remove the waffles** and place them on a wire rack to maintain crispness. Repeat with the remaining batter.
8. **Serve warm** with your favorite toppings such as maple syrup, whipped cream, or extra blueberries.

Nutritional Values (per serving): Calories: 320 | Protein: 8g | Carbohydrates: 45g | Dietary Fiber: 2g | Sugars: 12g | Fat: 12g | Saturated Fat: 6g | Cholesterol: 85mg | Sodium: 420mg.

CHEESY SOURDOUGH BREAKFAST BISCUITS

Preparation time: 15 minutes
Cooking time: 20 minutes
Servings: 4

The picture is only demonstrative of the recipe.

Ingredients:

- 1 cup (8,50 oz/240 g) active sourdough starter (100% hydration)
- 1½ cups (6,40 oz/180 g) all-purpose flour
- 1 tablespoon (0,50 oz/12 g) baking powder
- ½ teaspoon (2.5 g) baking soda
- ½ teaspoon (2.5 g) salt
- ½ cup (4 oz/115 g) cold unsalted butter, cubed
- 1 cup (100 g) shredded cheddar cheese (or your favorite cheese)
- ½ cup (120 ml) whole milk or buttermi

Instructions:

1. **Preheat the oven** to 425°F (218°C). Line a baking sheet with parchment paper.
2. **Mix dry ingredients:** In a large bowl, whisk together the flour, baking powder, baking soda, and salt.
3. **Cut in the butter:** Add the cold, cubed butter and use a pastry cutter or your fingers to incorporate it until the mixture is crumbly, with pea-sized pieces of butter remaining.
4. **Add cheese and sourdough starter:** Stir in the shredded cheese, then add the sourdough starter and milk. Mix until just combined; don't overwork the dough.
5. **Shape the biscuits:** Turn the dough out onto a floured surface. Pat it into a rectangle about 1 inch (2.5 cm) thick. Fold the dough in half, then in half again to create layers. Gently pat it out again and cut out biscuits using a round cutter. Re-roll the scraps to make more biscuits.
6. **Bake:** Place the biscuits on the prepared baking sheet, slightly touching each other for a softer edge or spaced apart for a crisper edge. Bake for 15-20 minutes until golden brown.
7. **Cool and serve:** Let the biscuits cool slightly on a wire rack. Serve warm with butter, jam, or alongside your favorite breakfast dishes.

Nutritional Values (per serving): Calories: 320 | Fat: 18 g | Carbohydrates: 31 g | Fiber: 1 g | Protein: 8 g | Sodium: 560 mg | Cholesterol: 45 mg

CHOCOLATE CHIP SOURDOUGH SCONES

Preparation Time: 15 minutes
Cooking Time: 20 minutes
Servings: 4 people

The picture is only demonstrative of the recipe.

Ingredients:

- 1 ¾ cups (8 oz/220 g) all-purpose flour
- ¼ cup (1,80 oz/50 g) granulated sugar
- 1 tablespoon baking powder
- ½ teaspoon salt
- ½ cup (3,60/113 g) cold unsalted butter, cubed
- ½ cup(4 oz/120 g) sourdough starter discard (unfed)
- ¼ cup (60 ml) heavy cream, plus extra for brushing
- 1 teaspoon vanilla extract
- ½ cup (3 oz/90 g) semi-sweet chocolate chips

Instructions:

1. **Preheat the oven** to 400°F (200°C). Line a baking sheet with parchment paper.
2. **In a large bowl**, whisk together the flour, sugar, baking powder, and salt.
3. **Cut in the cold butter** using a pastry cutter or your fingers until the mixture resembles coarse crumbs.
4. **Stir in the chocolate chips**, ensuring they are evenly distributed.
5. **In a separate bowl**, mix the sourdough starter, heavy cream, and vanilla extract.
6. **Pour the wet ingredients** into the dry mixture and stir until just combined. Do not overmix.
7. **Turn the dough out** onto a lightly floured surface. Gently shape it into a 1-inch (2.5 cm) thick circle.
8. **Cut into 8 wedges** and place them on the prepared baking sheet.
9. **Brush the tops** with a little heavy cream for a golden finish.
10. **Bake for 18–20 minutes** until golden brown. Allow to cool on a wire rack before serving.

Nutritional Values (per serving): Calories: 360 | Fat: 20 g|Carbohydrates: 42 g | Protein: 5 g | Fiber: 2 g | Sugar: 17 g | Sodium: 320 mg

CINNAMON RAISIN SOURDOUGH TOAST

Preparation Time: 15 minutes (plus rising time)
Cooking Time: 35 minutes
Servings: 4 people

The picture is only demonstrative of the recipe.

Ingredients:

- 3 cups (13 oz/360 g) bread flour
- ½ cup (4,20 oz/120 g) sourdough starter discard (unfed)
- 1 cup (240 ml) warm water
- 2 tablespoons (1 oz/30 g) honey
- 1 teaspoon salt
- 1 tablespoon ground cinnamon
- ½ cup (2,80 oz/80 g) raisins
- 2 tablespoons (1 oz/28 g) unsalted butter, melted

Instructions:

1. **In a large bowl**, mix the sourdough starter, warm water, and honey until combined.
2. **Add the flour, salt, and cinnamon** to the wet mixture. Stir until a sticky dough forms.
3. **Fold in the raisins** evenly throughout the dough.
4. **Cover the bowl** with a damp towel and let it rest for 30 minutes.
5. **Perform 3 sets of stretch-and-folds** every 30 minutes, then cover and let the dough rise for 4 hours at room temperature.
6. **After the rise**, shape the dough into a loaf and place it in a greased 9x5 inch (23x13 cm) loaf pan.
7. **Cover and refrigerate overnight** (or for at least 8 hours) for a slow ferment that enhances flavor.
8. **Preheat the oven** to 375°F (190°C).
9. **Brush the top** with melted butter and bake for 35 minutes, or until golden brown and hollow-sounding when tapped.
10. **Cool on a wire rack** before slicing. Toast slices and serve warm with butter or cream cheese.

Nutritional Values (per serving): Calories: 280 | Fat: 5 g | Carbohydrates: 52 g | Protein: 6 g | Fiber: 3 g | Sugar: 12 g | Sodium: 250 mg

CRANBERRY ORANGE SOURDOUGH MUFFINS

Preparation Time: 15 minutes
Cooking Time: 20 minutes
Servings: 4 people

The picture is only demonstrative of the recipe.

Ingredients:

- 1 cup (4,50 oz/125 g) all-purpose flour
- ½ cup (3,50 oz/100 g) granulated sugar
- ½ teaspoon baking powder
- ½ teaspoon baking soda
- ¼ teaspoon salt
- ½ cup (4,20 oz/120 g) sourdough starter discard (unfed)
- ¼ cup (60 ml) freshly squeezed orange juice
- ¼ cup (60 ml) vegetable oil
- 1 large egg
- 1 tablespoon orange zest
- ½ cup (2,15 oz/60 g) dried cranberries
- 1 tablespoon coarse sugar (optional, for topping)

Instructions:

1. **Preheat the oven** to 375°F (190°C). Line a muffin tin with paper liners or grease it well.
2. **In a large bowl**, whisk together the flour, sugar, baking powder, baking soda, and salt.
3. **In a separate bowl**, mix the sourdough starter, orange juice, vegetable oil, egg, and orange zest until well combined.
4. **Pour the wet ingredients** into the dry mixture and stir until just combined. Do not overmix.
5. **Fold in the dried cranberries** gently to evenly distribute them.
6. **Spoon the batter** into the prepared muffin tin, filling each cup about three-quarters full.
7. **Sprinkle coarse sugar** on top of each muffin for added crunch (optional).
8. **Bake for 18–20 minutes** or until a toothpick inserted into the center comes out clean.
9. **Allow to cool** in the tin for 5 minutes before transferring to a wire rack to cool completely.

Nutritional Values (per serving): Calories: 280 | Fat: 11 g | Carbohydrates: 41 g | Protein: 4 g | Fiber: 2 g | Sugar: 20 g | Sodium: 220 mg

FLUFFY SOURDOUGH SCRAMBLED EGG WRAPS

Preparation Time: 10 minutes
Cooking Time: 10 minutes
Servings: 4 people

The picture is only demonstrative of the recipe.

Ingredients:

- 1 cup (8,50 oz/240 g) sourdough starter discard (unfed)
- ½ cup (120 ml) milk
- 2 large eggs
- 1 cup (4,50 oz/125 g) all-purpose flour
- ¼ teaspoon salt
- 1 tablespoon(15 ml) olive oil (for cooking)

For the filling:

- 4 large eggs, whisked
- ¼ cup (60 ml) milk
- 1 tablespoon (0,50 oz/14 g) unsalted butter
- ½ cup (1,80 oz/50 g) shredded cheddar cheese
- Salt and pepper to taste
- Fresh herbs (optional, for garnish)

Instructions:

1. **In a bowl, combine** the sourdough starter, milk, eggs, flour, and salt. Mix until smooth and lump-free.
2. **Heat a non-stick skillet** over medium heat and add a little olive oil.
3. **Pour about ¼ cup** of the batter into the skillet, swirling to spread it thinly like a crepe.
4. **Cook for 1-2 minutes** until the edges lift easily. Flip and cook for another 30 seconds. Repeat for all wraps.
5. **In a separate pan**, melt the butter over medium-low heat.
6. **Whisk the eggs with milk**, then pour into the pan, stirring gently to create fluffy curds. Season with salt and pepper.
7. **Divide the scrambled eggs** among the sourdough wraps, sprinkle with cheddar cheese, and roll them up.
8. **Garnish with fresh herbs** if desired and serve warm.

Nutritional Values (per serving): Calories: 310 | Fat: 18 g | Carbohydrates: 25 g | Protein: 14 g | Fiber: 1 g | Sugar: 4 g | Sodium: 410 mg

HONEY WALNUT SOURDOUGH GRANOLA BARS

Preparation Time: 10 minutes
Cooking Time: 25 minutes
Servings: 4 people

The picture is only demonstrative of the recipe.

Ingredients:

- 1 cup (8,50 oz/240 g) sourdough starter discard (unfed)
- 1 ½ cups (5,30 oz/150 g) rolled oats
- ½ cup (120 ml) honey
- ¼ cup (2,15 oz/60 g) unsalted butter, melted
- ½ cup (2,15 oz/60 g) chopped walnuts
- ¼ cup (1,50 oz/40 g) dried cranberries
- 1 teaspoon vanilla extract
- ½ teaspoon ground cinnamon
- ¼ teaspoon salt

Instructions:

1. **Preheat the oven** to 350°F (175°C). Line an 8x8 inch (20x20 cm) baking pan with parchment paper.
2. **In a large bowl**, mix the sourdough starter, honey, melted butter, and vanilla extract until well combined.
3. **Stir in the rolled oats, walnuts, cranberries, cinnamon, and salt**, mixing until everything is evenly coated.
4. **Press the mixture** firmly into the prepared baking pan, ensuring an even layer.
5. **Bake for 20-25 minutes** or until golden brown around the edges.
6. **Remove from the oven** and let it cool completely in the pan before cutting into bars.
7. **Store in an airtight container** at room temperature for up to one week.

Nutritional Values (per serving): Calories: 320 | Fat: 16 g | Carbohydrates: 41 g | Protein: 5 g | Fiber: 3 g | Sugar: 20 g | Sodium: 150 mg

MAPLE PECAN SOURDOUGH COFFEE CAKE

Preparation Time: 15 minutes
Cooking Time: 35 minutes
Servings: 4 people

The picture is only demonstrative of the recipe.

Ingredients:

- **For the Cake:**
    - 1 cup (8,50 oz/240 g) sourdough starter discard (unfed)
    - 1 ½ cups (6,70 oz/190 g) all-purpose flour
    - ½ cup (120 ml) maple syrup
    - ¼ cup (60 ml) milk
    - ¼ cup (2,15 oz/60 g) unsalted butter, melted
    - 1 large egg
    - 1 teaspoon vanilla extract
    - 1 teaspoon baking powder
    - ½ teaspoon baking soda
    - ½ teaspoon ground cinnamon
    - ¼ teaspoon salt
- **For the Pecan Streusel Topping:**
    - ½ cup (1,80 oz/50 g) chopped pecans
    - ¼ cup (1,50/50 g) brown sugar
    - 2 tablespoons (1 oz/30 g) cold unsalted butter, cubed
    - 1 teaspoon ground cinnamon

Instructions:

1. **Preheat the oven** to 350°F (175°C). Grease an 8x8 inch (20x20 cm) baking pan or line it with parchment paper.
2. **In a large bowl**, mix the sourdough starter, maple syrup, milk, melted butter, egg, and vanilla extract until well combined.
3. **In a separate bowl**, whisk together the flour, baking powder, baking soda, cinnamon, and salt.

4. **Combine the dry and wet ingredients**, stirring until just incorporated. Do not overmix.
5. **Pour the batter** into the prepared baking pan, spreading it evenly.
6. **To make the streusel topping**, combine the chopped pecans, brown sugar, cinnamon, and cold butter. Use your fingers or a pastry cutter to mix until crumbly.
7. **Sprinkle the streusel** evenly over the cake batter.
8. **Bake for 30–35 minutes** or until a toothpick inserted into the center comes out clean.
9. **Cool in the pan** for 10 minutes before slicing and serving.

Nutritional Values (per serving): Calories: 380 | Fat: 18 g | Carbohydrates: 50 g | Protein: 5 g | Fiber: 2 g | Sugar: 25 g | Sodium: 320 mg.

PUMPKIN SPICE SOURDOUGH PANCAKES

Preparation Time: 10 minutes
Cooking Time: 15 minutes
Servings: 4 people

The picture is only demonstrative of the recipe.

Ingredients:

- 1 cup (8,50 oz/240 g) sourdough starter discard (unfed)
- 1 cup (240 ml) milk
- ½ cup (4,20 oz/120 g) canned pumpkin puree (not pumpkin pie filling)
- 1 large egg
- 2 tablespoons (1 oz/30 g) melted butter, plus extra for cooking
- 2 tablespoons (1 oz/30 g) brown sugar
- 1 teaspoon vanilla extract
- 1 ½ cups (6,70/190 g) all-purpose flour
- 2 teaspoons baking powder
- 1 teaspoon pumpkin pie spice
- ½ teaspoon ground cinnamon
- ¼ teaspoon salt

Instructions:

1. **In a large bowl**, combine the sourdough starter, milk, pumpkin puree, egg, melted butter, brown sugar, and vanilla extract. Whisk until smooth.
2. **In a separate bowl**, mix the flour, baking powder, pumpkin pie spice, cinnamon, and salt.
3. **Add the dry ingredients** to the wet mixture and stir until just combined. The batter should be slightly lumpy—do not overmix.
4. **Heat a non-stick skillet or griddle** over medium heat (about 350°F / 175°C). Lightly grease with butter.
5. **Pour ¼ cup** of batter onto the skillet for each pancake. Cook for about 2 minutes until bubbles form on the surface and the edges look set.
6. **Flip and cook** for another 1–2 minutes until golden brown and cooked through.
7. **Repeat with the remaining batter**, adding more butter to the skillet as needed.
8. **Serve warm**, topped with maple syrup, whipped cream, or chopped pecans if desired.

Nutritional Values (per serving): Calories: 310 | Fat: 11 g | Carbohydrates: 45 g | Protein: 6 g | Fiber: 2 g | Sugar: 15 g | Sodium: 350 mg

SOURDOUGH BREAKFAST FLATBREAD PIZZA

Preparation Time: 15 minutes
Cooking Time: 20 minutes
Servings: 4 people

The picture is only demonstrative of the recipe.

Ingredients:

- **For the Flatbread:**
  - 1 cup (8,50 oz/240 g) sourdough starter discard (unfed)
  - 1 cup (4,50 oz/125 g) all-purpose flour
  - ½ teaspoon baking powder
  - ½ teaspoon salt
  - 2 tablespoons (30 ml) olive oil
  - ¼ cup (60 ml) water (as needed to form a soft dough)
- **For the Toppings:**
  - ½ cup (120 ml) marinara sauce
  - 1 cup (3,50 oz/100 g) shredded mozzarella cheese
  - 4 large eggs
  - ½ cup (75 g) cherry tomatoes, halved
  - ¼ cup (1 oz/30 g) baby spinach
  - 1 tablespoon (0,60 oz/15 g) grated Parmesan cheese
  - Salt and pepper to taste
  - Fresh basil (optional, for garnish)

Instructions:

1. **Preheat the oven** to 425°F (220°C). Place a baking sheet or pizza stone inside to heat up.
2. **In a large bowl**, combine the sourdough starter, flour, baking powder, salt, and olive oil.
3. **Add water gradually**, mixing until a soft dough forms. If too sticky, add a little more flour.
4. **Divide the dough into 2 balls** and roll each out on a floured surface into thin flatbreads about ¼ inch (6 mm) thick.
5. **Carefully transfer** the flatbreads to a piece of parchment paper.

6. **Spread marinara sauce** evenly over each flatbread, leaving a small border around the edges.
7. **Sprinkle with mozzarella cheese**, then add cherry tomatoes and spinach.
8. **Crack an egg** onto each flatbread, seasoning with salt and pepper.
9. **Transfer the parchment paper** onto the preheated baking sheet or pizza stone.
10. **Bake for 15–20 minutes**, until the flatbreads are golden and the eggs are cooked to your liking.
11. **Remove from the oven** and sprinkle with Parmesan cheese and fresh basil if desired.
12. **Slice and serve warm**, enjoying the perfect blend of crispy flatbread, melty cheese, and savory breakfast toppings.

Nutritional Values (per serving): Calories: 350 | Fat: 18 g | Carbohydrates: 33 g | Protein: 14 g | Fiber: 2 g | Sugar: 5 g | Sodium: 540 mg

SOURDOUGH BREAKFAST QUESADILLAS

Preparation Time: 10 minutes
Cooking Time: 15 minutes
Servings: 4 people

The picture is only demonstrative of the recipe.

Ingredients:

- **For the Sourdough Tortillas:**
  - 1 cup (8,50 oz/240 g) sourdough-starter discard (unfed)
  - 1 cup (4,50 oz/125 g) all-purpose-flour
  - ¼ teaspoon baking powder
  - ½ teaspoon salt
  - 2 tablespoons (30 ml) olive oil
  - ¼ cup (60 ml) warm water (as needed)
- **For the Filling:**
  - 4 large eggs, scrambled
  - 1 cup (3,50 oz/100 g) shredded chedd cheese
  - ½ cup (2,60 oz/75 g) diced bell peppers (any color)
  - ½ cup (2,60 oz/75 g) diced cooked bacon or sausage (optional)
  - 2 tablespoons (1 oz/30 g) salsa (optional, for serving)
  - Fresh cilantro (optional, for garnish)

Instructions:

1. **In a bowl, mix** the sourdough starter, flour, baking powder, salt, and olive oil.
2. **Gradually add warm water** until a soft dough forms. If too sticky, add a little more flour.
3. **Divide the dough** into 4 equal balls and roll each out on a floured surface into thin tortillas.
4. **Heat a non-stick skillet** over medium-high heat. Cook each tortilla for 1–2 minutes on each side until lightly browned and puffy. Set aside.
5. **In the same skillet**, scramble the eggs and set aside.
6. **Assemble the quesadillas** by placing scrambled eggs, cheese, bell peppers, and cooked bacon or sausage on one half of each tortilla.
7. **Fold the tortillas in half** and return them to the skillet, cooking for 2–3 minutes per side until the cheese is melted and the tortillas are crispy.
8. **Slice into wedges** and serve warm with salsa and fresh cilantro if desired.

Nutritional Values (per serving): Calories: 340 | Fat: 18 g | Carbohydrates: 32 g | Protein: 14 g | Fiber: 2 g | Sugar: 3 g | Sodium: 480 mg

SOURDOUGH ENGLISH MUFFINS WITH AVOCADO SPREAD

Preparation Time: 20 minutes (plus 1 hour rising time)
Cooking Time: 15 minutes
Servings: 4 people

The picture is only demonstrative of the recipe.

Ingredients:

- **For the Sourdough English Muffins:**
  - 1 cup (8,50 oz/240 g) sourdough starter discard (unfed)
  - 1 ½ cups (6,70 oz/190 g) all-purpose flour
  - ½ cup (120 ml) warm milk
  - 1 tablespoon (0,50 oz/14 g) unsalted butter, melted
  - 1 tablespoon (0,50 oz/12 g) sugar
  - ½ teaspoon salt
  - ½ teaspoon baking soda
  - Cornmeal (for dusting)
- **For the Avocado Spread:**
  - 2 ripe avocados, mashed
  - 1 tablespoon (15 ml) lime juice
  - 1 clove garlic, minced
  - Salt and pepper to taste
  - Red pepper flakes (optional, for garnish)

Instructions:

1. **In a large bowl**, mix the sourdough starter, warm milk, melted butter, sugar, and salt until well combined.
2. **Add the flour and baking soda**, stirring until a sticky dough forms.
3. **Turn the dough out** onto a floured surface and knead gently for about 2 minutes until smooth.
4. **Roll the dough to about ½ inch (1.25 cm) thick** and use a round cutter to cut out 4–6 muffins.

5. **Dust each muffin** with cornmeal on both sides.
6. **Place the muffins** on a parchment-lined baking sheet, cover with a towel, and let rise for about 1 hour.
7. **Heat a non-stick skillet** over medium-low heat.
8. **Cook the muffins** for about 5–7 minutes per side, until golden brown and cooked through. Transfer to a wire rack to cool.
9. **For the avocado spread**, mix the mashed avocados, lime juice, garlic, salt, and pepper in a bowl until smooth.
10. **Slice the sourdough English muffins** in half and toast lightly.
11. **Spread the avocado mixture** generously on each half and sprinkle with red pepper flakes if desired.

Nutritional Values (per serving): Calories: 340 | Fat: 19 g | Carbohydrates: 37 g | Protein: 6 g | Fiber: 7 g | Sugar: 4 g | Sodium: 370 mg

APRICOT ALMOND SOURDOUGH BARS

Preparation Time: 15 minutes
Cooking Time: 25 minutes
Portions: Serves 4

The picture is only demonstrative of the recipe.

Ingredients:

- 1 cup sourdough discard (unfed)
- 1 cup rolled oats
- ½ cup almond flour
- ½ cup dried apricots, chopped
- ¼ cup honey (or maple syrup for a vegan option)
- ¼ cup almond butter
- ¼ cup sliced almonds (for topping)
- 1 teaspoon vanilla extract
- ½ teaspoon cinnamon
- ¼ teaspoon salt

Instructions:

1. **Preheat the Oven:** Preheat your oven to 350°F (175°C). Line an 8x8 inch baking pan with parchment paper, leaving some overhang for easy removal.
2. **Mix Wet Ingredients:** In a large bowl, combine sourdough discard, honey, almond butter, and vanilla extract. Stir until smooth and well incorporated.
3. **Add Dry Ingredients:** Fold in the oats, almond flour, cinnamon, and salt. Mix until a thick, sticky batter forms. Stir in the chopped apricots.
4. **Spread and Top:** Transfer the mixture to the prepared baking pan, pressing it down evenly with a spatula. Sprinkle sliced almonds on top, pressing them lightly into the surface.
5. **Bake:** Place the pan in the preheated oven and bake for 25 minutes or until the edges are golden brown.
6. **Cool and Slice:** Allow the bars to cool completely in the pan before lifting them out using the parchment overhang. Slice into bars and serve.

Nutritional Values (per serving): Calories: 220 | Protein: 5g | Carbohydrates: 30g | Fat: 10g | Fiber: 4g | Sugar: 12g

BBQ SOURDOUGH POPCORN CROUTONS

Preparation Time: 10 minutes
Cooking Time: 20 minutes
Portions: Serves 4

The picture is only demonstrative of the recipe.

Ingredients:

- 2 cups sourdough discard (unfed)
- 1 cup popcorn kernels, popped and lightly crushed
- ¼ cup olive oil
- 2 tablespoons BBQ seasoning (sugar-free for a healthier option)
- 1 teaspoon smoked paprika
- ½ teaspoon garlic powder
- ½ teaspoon onion powder
- ½ teaspoon salt
- ¼ teaspoon black pepper

Instructions:

1. **Preheat the Oven:** Preheat your oven to 375°F (190°C). Line a baking sheet with parchment paper.
2. **Mix the Base:** In a large bowl, combine the sourdough discard and olive oil. Stir until smooth and well blended.
3. **Season and Fold:** Add the BBQ seasoning, smoked paprika, garlic powder, onion powder, salt, and black pepper. Mix well. Fold in the lightly crushed popcorn kernels until evenly coated.
4. **Spread and Bake:** Spread the mixture evenly on the prepared baking sheet, flattening it to about ¼ inch thickness. Bake for 15-20 minutes, or until crispy and golden brown, flipping halfway through for even cooking.
5. **Cool and Break Apart:** Allow the croutons to cool completely before breaking them into bite-sized pieces. Store in an airtight container for up to one week.

Nutritional Values (per serving): Calories: 190 | Protein: 4g | Carbohydrates: 22g | Fat: 9g | Fiber: 3g | Sugar: 1g

CARAMELIZED ONION SOURDOUGH PINWHEELS

Preparation Time: 20 minutes
Cooking Time: 25 minutes
Portions: Serves 4

The picture is only demonstrative of the recipe.

Ingredients:

- 1 cup sourdough discard (unfed)
- 1½ cups all-purpose flour
- ½ cup unsalted butter, cold and cubed
- 1 large onion, thinly sliced
- 2 tablespoons olive oil
- 1 tablespoon balsamic vinegar
- 1 teaspoon dried thyme
- ½ teaspoon salt
- ¼ teaspoon black pepper
- ½ cup shredded mozzarella cheese
- 1 egg, beaten (for egg wash)

Instructions:

1. **Caramelize the Onions:** In a skillet, heat olive oil over medium heat. Add sliced onions, salt, and pepper. Cook, stirring occasionally, until golden and caramelized (about 15 minutes). Stir in balsamic vinegar and thyme. Remove from heat and let cool.
2. **Prepare the Dough:** In a large bowl, combine sourdough discard and cold butter. Cut the butter into the flour using a pastry cutter or fork until crumbly. Add flour and mix until a dough forms.
3. **Roll and Fill:** On a floured surface, roll out the dough into a rectangle (about ¼ inch thick). Spread the caramelized onions evenly over the dough, leaving a small border around the edges. Sprinkle shredded mozzarella cheese on top.
4. **Shape the Pinwheels:** Roll up the dough tightly from the long side, sealing the edges with a bit of water. Slice the roll into 1-inch pieces and place them on a parchment-lined baking sheet.
5. **Bake:** Preheat your oven to 375°F (190°C). Brush the pinwheels with beaten egg for a golden finish. Bake for 20-25 minutes or until golden brown and crispy.
6. **Cool and Serve:** Allow the pinwheels to cool slightly before serving warm or at room temperature.

Nutritional Values (per serving): Calories: 280 | Protein: 6g | Carbohydrates: 28g | Fat: 16g | Fiber: 2g | Sugar: 3g

CHOCOLATE HAZELNUT SOURDOUGH DIP STICKS

Preparation Time: 15 minutes (plus 1 hour resting time)
Cooking Time: 20 minutes
Portions: Serves 4

The picture is only demonstrative of the recipe.

Ingredients:

- 1 cup sourdough discard (unfed)
- 1½ cups all-purpose flour
- ¼ cup cocoa powder (unsweetened)
- ¼ cup hazelnut flour (or finely ground hazelnuts)
- ¼ cup honey or maple syrup
- ¼ cup olive oil
- 1 teaspoon vanilla extract
- ½ teaspoon salt
- ½ cup dark chocolate chips (for dipping)
- ¼ cup chopped hazelnuts (for garnish)

Instructions:

1. **Make the Dough:** In a large bowl, combine sourdough discard, honey, olive oil, and vanilla extract. Stir until well mixed.
2. **Add Dry Ingredients:** Add all-purpose flour, cocoa powder, hazelnut flour, and salt. Mix until a sticky dough forms.
3. **Rest the Dough:** Cover the bowl and let the dough rest at room temperature for 1 hour to allow the flavors to meld and the dough to relax.
4. **Shape the Sticks:** Preheat your oven to 375°F (190°C). Divide the dough into small portions and roll each one into thin sticks, about 6 inches long. Place on a parchment-lined baking sheet, leaving space between each stick.
5. **Bake:** Bake for 15-20 minutes or until firm and slightly crispy. Let them cool completely on a wire rack.
6. **Dip and Garnish:** Melt the dark chocolate chips in a microwave-safe bowl in 20-second intervals, stirring in between until smooth. Dip one end of each sourdough stick into the melted chocolate, then sprinkle with chopped hazelnuts. Let the chocolate set before serving.

Nutritional Values (per serving): Calories: 250 | Protein: 4g | Carbohydrates: 32g | Fat: 12g | Fiber: 3g | Sugar: 15g

SOURDOUGH BREADSTICKS

Preparation Time: 20 minutes (plus 1 hour rising time)
Cooking Time: 20 minutes
Portions: Serves 4

The picture is only demonstrative of the recipe.

Ingredients:

- 1 cup sourdough discard (unfed)
- 1½ cups all-purpose flour
- ½ cup grated Parmesan cheese
- ¼ cup olive oil (plus extra for brushing)
- 2 cloves garlic, minced
- 1 teaspoon dried oregano
- 1 teaspoon salt
- ½ teaspoon black pepper
- ½ teaspoon garlic powder
- ½ teaspoon dried basil
- Optional: sauce for dipping

Instructions:

1. **Make the Dough:** In a large bowl, combine sourdough discard, olive oil, minced garlic, and salt. Gradually add flour, mixing until a soft, slightly sticky dough forms.
2. **Knead and Rise:** Turn the dough onto a floured surface and knead for about 5 minutes until smooth and elastic. Place in a greased bowl, cover, and let rise in a warm place for 1 hour.
3. **Shape the Breadsticks:** Preheat your oven to 400°F (205°C). Divide the dough into 12 equal pieces. Roll each piece into a long rope, about 8 inches long, and place on a parchment-lined baking sheet.
4. **Season and Bake:** In a small bowl, mix Parmesan cheese, garlic powder, oregano, basil, and black pepper. Brush each breadstick with olive oil and sprinkle generously with the Parmesan mixture.
5. **Bake:** Bake for 15-20 minutes or until golden brown and crispy.
6. **Cool and Serve:** Allow the breadsticks to cool slightly before serving warm with marinara sauce for dipping.

Nutritional Values (per serving): Calories: 250 | Protein: 7g | Carbohydrates: 28g | Fat: 12g | Fiber: 2g | Sugar: 1g

HERBED SOURDOUGH MINI PITA CHIPS

Preparation Time: 15 minutes
Cooking Time: 20 minutes
Portions: Serves 4

The picture is only demonstrative of the recipe.

Ingredients:

- 1 cup sourdough discard (unfed)
- 1½ cups all-purpose flour
- ¼ cup olive oil (plus extra for brushing)
- 1 teaspoon dried oregano
- 1 teaspoon dried thyme
- 1 teaspoon garlic powder
- ½ teaspoon salt
- ½ teaspoon black pepper
- ¼ teaspoon smoked paprika (optional, for extra flavor)
- Optional: Hummus or Greek yogurt dip for serving

Instructions:

1. **Make the Dough:** In a large bowl, mix sourdough discard, olive oil, salt, and garlic powder. Gradually add flour until a soft, slightly sticky dough forms.
2. **Rest the Dough:** Cover the bowl and let the dough rest for 30 minutes at room temperature to develop flavor.
3. **Shape the Pitas:** Preheat your oven to 400°F (205°C). Divide the dough into small portions and roll each one into a circle about 4 inches in diameter. Place on a parchment-lined baking sheet.
4. **Season and Cut:** In a small bowl, combine oregano, thyme, black pepper, and smoked paprika. Brush each pita circle with olive oil and sprinkle with the herb mixture. Using a pizza cutter, cut each circle into 4 wedges.
5. **Bake:** Bake for 15-20 minutes or until golden and crispy, flipping halfway through for even browning.
6. **Cool and Serve:** Allow the pita chips to cool completely before serving with hummus or Greek yogurt dip.

Nutritional Values (per serving): Calories: 210 | Protein: 5g | Carbohydrates: 28g | Fat: 9g | Fiber: 2g | Sugar: 1g

JALAPEÑO CHEDDAR SOURDOUGH NUGGETS

Preparation Time: 20 minutes (plus 1 hour rising time)
Cooking Time: 20 minutes
Portions: Serves 4

The picture is only demonstrative of the recipe.

Ingredients:

- 1 cup sourdough discard (unfed)
- 1½ cups all-purpose flour
- 1 cup sharp cheddar cheese, shredded
- 1 jalapeño, finely chopped (seeds removed for less heat)
- ¼ cup warm water
- 2 tablespoons olive oil (plus extra for brushing)
- 1 teaspoon salt
- ½ teaspoon garlic powder
- ½ teaspoon smoked paprika
- Optional: Ranch or sour cream for dipping

Instructions:

1. **Make the Dough:** In a large bowl, combine sourdough discard, warm water, olive oil, and salt. Gradually add flour, mixing until a soft, slightly sticky dough forms.
2. **Add Flavor:** Fold in shredded cheddar cheese, chopped jalapeño, garlic powder, and smoked paprika until evenly distributed throughout the dough.
3. **Knead and Rise:** Turn the dough onto a floured surface and knead for about 5 minutes until smooth and elastic. Place in a greased bowl, cover, and let rise in a warm place for 1 hour.
4. **Shape the Nuggets:** Preheat your oven to 400°F (205°C). Divide the dough into small, bite-sized pieces and shape into nuggets. Place on a parchment-lined baking sheet.
5. **Brush and Bake:** Brush the nuggets lightly with olive oil for a golden finish. Bake for 15-20 minutes, or until puffed and golden brown.
6. **Cool and Serve:** Allow the nuggets to cool slightly before serving warm with ranch or sour cream for dipping.

Nutritional Values (per serving): Calories: 240 | Protein: 7g | Carbohydrates: 28g | Fat: 11g | Fiber: 2g | Sugar: 1g

LOADED SOURDOUGH POTATO SKINS

Preparation Time: 15 minutes
Cooking Time: 30 minutes
Portions: Serves 4

The picture is only demonstrative of the recipe.

Ingredients:

- 4 medium russet potatoes, scrubbed and halved
- 1 cup sourdough discard (unfed)
- 1 cup shredded cheddar cheese
- ½ cup sour cream (plus extra for serving)
- ½ cup cooked bacon, crumbled
- ¼ cup green onions, chopped
- 2 tablespoons olive oil
- 1 teaspoon garlic powder
- ½ teaspoon smoked paprika
- ½ teaspoon salt
- ¼ teaspoon black pepper

Instructions:

1. **Prepare the Potatoes:** Preheat your oven to 425°F (220°C). Scoop out most of the potato flesh, leaving a thin layer to maintain structure. Save the scooped potato for another use.
2. **Season and Bake:** Place the potato skins on a baking sheet, brush with olive oil, and sprinkle with salt, pepper, garlic powder, and smoked paprika. Bake for 15 minutes until crispy.
3. **Fill with Sourdough Mixture:** In a bowl, mix sourdough discard, half of the cheddar cheese, and sour cream until smooth. Spoon the mixture evenly into each potato skin.
4. **Top and Finish Baking:** Sprinkle the remaining cheddar cheese and crumbled bacon on top. Return to the oven and bake for another 10-15 minutes until the cheese is melted and bubbly.
5. **Garnish and Serve:** Remove from the oven and top with chopped green onions. Serve hot with extra sour cream on the side.

Nutritional Values (per serving): Calories: 320 | Protein: 10g | Carbohydrates: 28g | Fat: 18g | Fiber: 3g | Sugar: 2g

MINI SOURDOUGH PIZZA BITES

Preparation Time: 20 minutes (plus 30 minutes resting time)
Cooking Time: 15 minutes
Portions: Serves 4

The picture is only demonstrative of the recipe.

Ingredients:

- 1 cup sourdough discard (unfed)
- 1½ cups all-purpose flour
- ½ cup warm water
- 2 tablespoons olive oil (plus extra for brushing)
- ½ teaspoon salt
- ½ teaspoon garlic powder
- ½ teaspoon dried oregano
- 1 cup marinara sauce
- 1 cup shredded mozzarella cheese
- ¼ cup mini pepperoni slices (or chopped veggies for a vegetarian option)
- Optional: Red pepper flakes and fresh basil for garnish

Instructions:

1. **Make the Dough:** In a large bowl, combine sourdough discard, warm water, olive oil, salt, garlic powder, and oregano. Gradually add flour, mixing until a soft, slightly sticky dough forms.
2. **Rest the Dough:** Cover the bowl and let the dough rest for 30 minutes at room temperature to develop flavor.
3. **Shape the Pizza Bites:** Preheat your oven to 425°F (220°C). Divide the dough into small portions and roll each into a ball. Flatten each ball slightly and place on a parchment-lined baking sheet.
4. **Add Toppings:** Using your fingers, make a small indentation in the center of each dough ball. Spoon a little marinara sauce into the indentation and top with shredded mozzarella and mini pepperoni slices.
5. **Bake:** Brush the edges of each pizza bite with olive oil for a golden finish. Bake for 12-15 minutes, or until the cheese is melted and bubbly and the dough is golden brown.
6. **Cool and Serve:** Allow the pizza bites to cool slightly before serving warm. Garnish with red pepper flakes and fresh basil if desired.

Nutritional Values (per serving): Calories: 260 | Protein: 8g | Carbohydrates: 32g | Fat: 10g | Fiber: 2g | Sugar: 3g

PEANUT BUTTER SOURDOUGH ENERGY BALLS

Preparation Time: 15 minutes
Cooking Time: None (chilling time: 30 minutes)
Portions: Serves 4

The picture is only demonstrative of the recipe.

Ingredients:

- ½ cup sourdough discard (unfed)
- ½ cup creamy peanut butter (natural, no added sugar)
- ½ cup rolled oats
- ¼ cup honey (or maple syrup for a vegan option)
- ¼ cup dark chocolate chips
- 2 tablespoons chia seeds
- 1 teaspoon vanilla extract
- ½ teaspoon cinnamon
- Pinch of salt

Instructions:

1. **Combine Wet Ingredients:** In a large bowl, mix sourdough discard, peanut butter, honey, and vanilla extract until smooth and well combined.
2. **Add Dry Ingredients:** Stir in rolled oats, chia seeds, cinnamon, and salt until evenly incorporated. Fold in dark chocolate chips.
3. **Shape the Energy Balls:** Using your hands or a small cookie scoop, form the mixture into bite-sized balls, about 1 inch in diameter. Place them on a parchment-lined baking sheet.
4. **Chill and Set:** Refrigerate for at least 30 minutes to firm up.
5. **Serve and Store:** Enjoy immediately or store in an airtight container in the refrigerator for up to one week.

Nutritional Values (per serving): Calories: 210 | Protein: 6g | Carbohydrates: 22g | Fat: 12g | Fiber: 4g | Sugar: 10g

PUMPKIN CHOCOLATE CHIP SOURDOUGH BARS

Preparation Time: 15 minutes
Cooking Time: 25 minutes
Portions: Serves 4

The picture is only demonstrative of the recipe.

Ingredients:

- 1 cup sourdough discard (unfed)
- 1 cup canned pumpkin puree (not pumpkin pie filling)
- ½ cup coconut sugar (or brown sugar)
- ½ cup melted coconut oil (or unsalted butter)
- 1 teaspoon vanilla extract
- 1½ cups all-purpose flour
- 1 teaspoon baking powder
- 1 teaspoon pumpkin pie spice
- ½ teaspoon cinnamon
- ½ teaspoon salt
- ¾ cup dark chocolate chips

Instructions:

1. **Preheat the Oven:** Preheat your oven to 350°F (175°C). Line an 8x8 inch baking pan with parchment paper, leaving some overhang for easy removal.
2. **Mix Wet Ingredients:** In a large bowl, combine sourdough discard, pumpkin puree, melted coconut oil, coconut sugar, and vanilla extract. Stir until smooth.
3. **Add Dry Ingredients:** Add flour, baking powder, pumpkin pie spice, cinnamon, and salt. Mix until a thick batter forms. Fold in the dark chocolate chips.
4. **Spread and Bake:** Spread the batter evenly in the prepared baking pan. Smooth the top with a spatula. Bake for 25 minutes or until a toothpick inserted into the center comes out clean.
5. **Cool and Slice:** Allow the bars to cool completely in the pan before lifting them out using the parchment overhang. Slice into bars and serve.

Nutritional Values (per serving): Calories: 260 | Protein: 4g | Carbohydrates: 36g | Fat: 12g | Fiber: 3g | Sugar: 18g

SAVORY SOURDOUGH PANCAKE DIPPERS

Preparation Time: 10 minutes
Cooking Time: 15 minutes
Portions: Serves 4

The picture is only demonstrative of the recipe.

Ingredients:

- 1 cup sourdough discard (unfed)
- ½ cup all-purpose flour
- ½ cup milk (dairy or non-dairy)
- 1 large egg
- ¼ cup shredded cheddar cheese
- ¼ cup cooked bacon, crumbled (optional)
- 2 tablespoons chopped chives
- 1 teaspoon garlic powder
- ½ teaspoon salt
- ¼ teaspoon black pepper
- Olive oil or butter for cooking
- Optional: Ranch or marinara sauce for dipping

Instructions:

1. **Make the Batter:** In a large bowl, whisk together sourdough discard, milk, and egg until smooth. Stir in flour, garlic powder, salt, and black pepper until just combined. Fold in shredded cheddar cheese, crumbled bacon, and chopped chives.
2. **Heat the Pan:** Heat a non-stick skillet or griddle over medium heat. Lightly grease with olive oil or butter.
3. **Cook the Pancake Dippers:** Drop spoonfuls of batter onto the skillet, forming oval shapes about 3 inches long for easy dipping. Cook for 2-3 minutes on each side, or until golden brown and cooked through.
4. **Serve:** Transfer to a plate lined with paper towels to absorb any excess oil. Serve warm with ranch or marinara sauce for dipping.

Nutritional Values (per serving): Calories: 220 | Protein: 8g | Carbohydrates: 22g | Fat: 11g | Fiber: 1g | Sugar: 2g

SOURDOUGH APPLE PIE ROLL-UPS

Preparation Time: 15 minutes
Cooking Time: 20 minutes
Portions: Serves 4

The picture is only demonstrative of the recipe.

Ingredients:

- 1 cup sourdough discard (unfed)
- 1½ cups all-purpose flour
- ¼ cup unsalted butter, melted
- 2 medium apples (Granny Smith or Honeycrisp), peeled and thinly sliced
- ¼ cup coconut sugar (or brown sugar)
- 1 teaspoon cinnamon
- ¼ teaspoon nutmeg
- 1 teaspoon vanilla extract
- 1 tablespoon lemon juice
- 1 egg, beaten (for egg wash)
- Optional: Powdered sugar for dusting

Instructions:

1. **Make the Dough:** In a large bowl, combine sourdough discard, melted butter, and vanilla extract. Gradually add flour, mixing until a soft, slightly sticky dough forms.
2. **Prepare the Apple Filling:** In a separate bowl, mix sliced apples with coconut sugar, cinnamon, nutmeg, and lemon juice until evenly coated.
3. **Shape the Roll-Ups:** Preheat your oven to 375°F (190°C). Roll out the dough on a floured surface into a large rectangle (about ¼ inch thick). Cut into 4 smaller rectangles. Arrange the apple slices in a single layer on each rectangle.
4. **Roll and Seal:** Roll up each rectangle tightly, sealing the edges by pinching the dough together. Place seam-side down on a parchment-lined baking sheet. Brush with beaten egg for a golden finish.
5. **Bake:** Bake for 20 minutes or until golden brown and crispy.
6. **Cool and Serve:** Allow to cool slightly before dusting with powdered sugar (optional). Serve warm or at room temperature.

Nutritional Values (per serving): Calories: 250 | Protein: 4g | Carbohydrates: 36g | Fat: 10g | Fiber: 3g | Sugar: 15g

SOURDOUGH GARLIC PARMESAN KNOTS

Preparation Time: 20 minutes (plus 1 hour rising time)
Cooking Time: 20 minutes
Portions: Serves 4

The picture is only demonstrative of the recipe.

Ingredients:

- 1 cup sourdough discard (unfed)
- 1½ cups all-purpose flour
- ¼ cup warm water
- 2 tablespoons olive oil (plus extra for brushing)
- 1 teaspoon salt
- 1 teaspoon garlic powder
- ½ teaspoon dried oregano
- ½ teaspoon dried basil
- ½ cup grated Parmesan cheese
- 2 cloves garlic, minced
- 2 tablespoons fresh parsley, chopped (for garnish)
- Optional: Marinara sauce for dipping

Instructions:

1. **Make the Dough:** In a large bowl, combine sourdough discard, warm water, olive oil, salt, and garlic powder. Gradually add flour, mixing until a soft, slightly sticky dough forms.
2. **Knead and Rise:** Turn the dough onto a floured surface and knead for about 5 minutes until smooth and elastic. Place in a greased bowl, cover, and let rise in a warm place for 1 hour.
3. **Shape the Knots:** Preheat your oven to 400°F (205°C). Divide the dough into small portions and roll each one into a rope about 6 inches long. Tie each rope into a knot and place on a parchment-lined baking sheet.
4. **Season and Bake:** In a small bowl, mix minced garlic and olive oil. Brush the knots with the garlic oil mixture and sprinkle with grated Parmesan cheese, oregano, and basil. Bake for 15-20 minutes, or until golden brown and crispy.
5. **Garnish and Serve:** Remove from the oven and sprinkle with fresh parsley. Serve warm with marinara sauce for dipping.

Nutritional Values (per serving): Calories: 230 | Protein: 6g | Carbohydrates: 28g | Fat: 10g | Fiber: 2g | Sugar: 1g

BBQ SOURDOUGH CHICKEN FLATBREADS

Preparation Time: 15 minutes
Cooking Time: 20 minutes
Servings: Serves 4

The picture is only demonstrative of the recipe.

Ingredients:

- 1 cup sourdough discard (unfed)
- 1½ cups all-purpose flour
- ½ cup warm water
- 2 tablespoons olive oil (plus extra for brushing)
- 1 teaspoon garlic powder
- ½ teaspoon salt
- 2 cups cooked chicken, shredded (rotisserie chicken works great)
- ½ cup BBQ sauce (use your favorite brand)
- 1 cup shredded cheddar cheese
- ½ red onion, thinly sliced
- ¼ cup chopped fresh cilantro (for garnish)
- Optional: Red pepper flakes for extra heat

Instructions:

1. **Make the Flatbread Dough:** In a large bowl, combine sourdough discard, warm water, olive oil, salt, and garlic powder. Gradually add flour, mixing until a soft, slightly sticky dough forms. Knead for about 5 minutes until smooth.
2. **Shape and Pre-Cook:** Divide the dough into 4 equal portions. Roll each portion into a thin oval or round shape. Heat a large skillet or griddle over medium-high heat and brush with olive oil. Cook each flatbread for about 2 minutes per side until lightly golden but still soft.
3. **Assemble the Flatbreads:** Preheat your oven to 425°F (220°C). Place the pre-cooked flatbreads on a baking sheet. In a bowl, mix shredded chicken with BBQ sauce. Spread the chicken mixture evenly over each flatbread. Top with shredded cheddar cheese and sliced red onion.
4. **Bake:** Bake for about 8-10 minutes, or until the cheese is melted and bubbly.
5. **Garnish and Serve:** Remove from the oven and sprinkle with fresh cilantro. Add red pepper flakes if desired. Serve hot and enjoy!

Nutritional Values (per serving): Calories: 390 | Protein: 25g | Carbohydrates: 42g | Fat: 14g | Fiber: 2g | Sugar: 9g

CHEESY SOURDOUGH STUFFED PEPPERS

Preparation Time: 15 minutes
Cooking Time: 30 minutes
Servings: Serves 4

The picture is only demonstrative of the recipe.

Ingredients:

- 1 cup sourdough discard (unfed)
- 4 large bell peppers (any color), tops cut off and seeds removed
- 1 cup cooked quinoa (or rice)
- 1 cup shredded cheddar cheese
- ½ cup sourdough breadcrumbs (from stale sourdough bread, finely crushed)
- 1 cup diced tomatoes (canned or fresh)
- ½ cup black beans, drained and rinsed
- 1 teaspoon garlic powder
- 1 teaspoon dried oregano
- ½ teaspoon smoked paprika
- ½ teaspoon salt
- ¼ teaspoon black pepper
- 2 tablespoons olive oil (for drizzling)
- Optional: Chopped fresh parsley for garnish

Instructions:

1. **Prepare the Filling:** Preheat your oven to 375°F (190°C). In a large bowl, combine sourdough discard, cooked quinoa, diced tomatoes, black beans, garlic powder, oregano, smoked paprika, salt, and black pepper. Stir until well mixed.
2. **Stuff the Peppers:** Arrange the hollowed-out bell peppers in a baking dish. Fill each pepper with the sourdough mixture, pressing down slightly to pack it in. Top each with shredded cheddar cheese and a sprinkle of sourdough breadcrumbs.
3. **Bake:** Drizzle the peppers with olive oil and cover the baking dish with foil. Bake for 25 minutes. Remove the foil and bake for an additional 5 minutes, or until the cheese is melted and golden.
4. **Garnish and Serve:** Remove from the oven and let cool slightly. Garnish with chopped fresh parsley, if desired. Serve hot as a delicious and satisfying main dish.

Nutritional Values (per serving): Calories: 320 | Protein: 12g | Carbohydrates: 42g | Fat: 12g | Fiber: 8g | Sugar: 8g

CREAMY SOURDOUGH FANTASY PASTA

Preparation Time: 15 minutes
Cooking Time: 20 minutes
Servings: Serves 4

The picture is only demonstrative of the recipe.

Ingredients:

- 1 cup sourdough discard (unfed)
- 12 oz pasta (penne or fusilli or whatever pasta you like to cookpasta to taste)
- 1 cup heavy cream (or coconut cream for a dairy-free option)
- ½ cup sourdough breadcrumbs (from stale sourdough bread, finely crushed)
- 1 cup grated Parmesan cheese
- 1 cup baby spinach, chopped
- 1 cup cherry tomatoes, halved
- 3 cloves garlic, minced
- 2 tablespoons olive oil
- 1 teaspoon dried basil
- ½ teaspoon red pepper flakes (optional, for a spicy kick)
- Salt and black pepper to taste
- Optional: Fresh basil leaves for garnish

Instructions:

1. **Cook the Pasta:** Cook the pasta in a large pot of salted boiling water according to package instructions. Drain and set aside.
2. **Make the Creamy Sourdough Sauce:** In a large skillet, heat olive oil over medium heat. Add minced garlic and cook until fragrant. Stir in sourdough discard, heavy cream, and dried basil. Simmer for 2-3 minutes until slightly thickened.
3. **Combine and Season:** Add the cooked pasta, chopped spinach, cherry tomatoes, Parmesan cheese, salt, and black pepper. Stir until the pasta is well coated and the spinach is wilted.
4. **Add Crunchy Topping:** In a small pan, toast the sourdough breadcrumbs with a drizzle of olive oil until golden and crispy. Sprinkle over the pasta for extra crunch.
5. **Serve:** Plate the pasta and garnish with fresh basil leaves. Serve hot and enjoy the creamy, tangy goodness.

Nutritional Values (per serving): Calories: 420 | Protein: 12g | Carbohydrates: 58g | Fat: 16g | Fiber: 4g | Sugar: 6g

CRISPY SOURDOUGH FISH TACOS

Preparation Time: 15 minutes
Cooking Time: 15 minutes
Servings: Serves 4

The picture is only demonstrative of the recipe.

Ingredients:

- 1 cup sourdough discard (unfed)
- 1 pound white fish fillets (cod or tilapia), cut into strips
- 1 cup sourdough breadcrumbs (from stale sourdough bread, finely crushed)
- ½ cup cornmeal (for extra crunch)
- 1 teaspoon smoked paprika
- 1 teaspoon garlic powder
- ½ teaspoon cumin
- ½ teaspoon salt
- ½ teaspoon black pepper
- 1 large egg, beaten
- Olive oil spray (for baking)
- 8 small corn tortillas
- 1 cup shredded cabbage
- ½ cup sour cream
- 1 tablespoon lime juice
- ¼ cup chopped cilantro (for garnish)
- Optional: Sliced jalapeños for heat

Instructions:

1. **Prepare the Coating:** Preheat your oven to 425°F (220°C). In a shallow bowl, combine sourdough breadcrumbs, cornmeal, smoked paprika, garlic powder, cumin, salt, and black pepper.
2. **Coat the Fish:** Dip each fish strip into the sourdough discard, letting any excess drip off. Then dip into the beaten egg, followed by the breadcrumb mixture, pressing lightly to coat.
3. **Bake the Fish:** Place the coated fish strips on a parchment-lined baking sheet. Lightly spray with olive oil for extra crispiness. Bake for 15 minutes, flipping halfway through, until golden and crispy.
4. **Prepare the Toppings:** In a small bowl, mix sour cream with lime juice for a zesty crema. Warm the corn tortillas in a dry skillet over medium heat until pliable.
5. **Assemble the Tacos:** Place crispy fish strips on each tortilla. Top with shredded cabbage, lime crema, and chopped cilantro. Add sliced jalapeños if desired.
6. **Serve:** Serve hot with lime wedges on the side for extra zing.

Nutritional Values (per serving): Calories: 320 | Protein: 22g | Carbohydrates: 34g | Fat: 11g | Fiber: 4g | Sugar: 3g

HEARTY SOURDOUGH VEGGIE BURGERS

Preparation Time: 15 minutes
Cooking Time: 15 minutes
Servings: Serves 4

The picture is only demonstrative of the recipe.

Ingredients:

- 1 cup sourdough discard (unfed)
- 1 can (15 oz / 425 g) black beans, drained and mashed
- 1 cup shredded carrots (about 110 g)
- ½ cup sourdough breadcrumbs (from stale sourdough bread, finely crushed)
- ¼ cup chopped red onion (about 40 g)
- ¼ cup chopped fresh parsley (about 15 g)
- 1 teaspoon garlic powder
- 1 teaspoon smoked paprika
- ½ teaspoon cumin
- ½ teaspoon salt
- ¼ teaspoon black pepper
- 1 large egg, beaten
- 2 tablespoons olive oil (for frying)
- 4 sourdough burger buns, toasted
- Optional Toppings: Sliced avocado, lettuce, tomato, pickles, mustard, or ketchup

Instructions:

1. **Make the Veggie Patty Mixture:** In a large bowl, combine sourdough discard, mashed black beans, shredded carrots, red onion, parsley, garlic powder, smoked paprika, cumin, salt, and black pepper. Stir in the beaten egg and sourdough breadcrumbs, mixing until well combined.
2. **Shape the Patties:** Divide the mixture into 4 equal portions and shape each into a patty about ½ inch thick.
3. **Cook the Patties:** Heat olive oil in a large skillet over medium heat. Cook the patties for about 4-5 minutes per side, or until golden brown and crispy on the outside.
4. **Assemble the Burgers:** Place each patty on a toasted sourdough bun. Add desired toppings such as sliced avocado, lettuce, tomato, and condiments like mustard or ketchup.
5. **Serve:** Serve hot with a side of sweet potato fries or a fresh salad for a complete meal.

Nutritional Values (per serving): Calories: 320 | Protein: 12g | Carbohydrates: 48g | Fat: 10g | Fiber: 8g | Sugar: 4g

HONEY MUSTARD SOURDOUGH CHICKEN BITES

Preparation Time: 15 minutes
Cooking Time: 20 minutes
Servings: Serves 4

The picture is only demonstrative of the recipe.

Ingredients:

- 1 cup sourdough discard (unfed)
- 1 lb (16 oz / 450 g) chicken breast, cut into bite-sized pieces
- ½ cup sourdough breadcrumbs (from stale sourdough bread, finely crushed)
- ¼ cup honey (3 oz / 85 g)
- ¼ cup Dijon mustard (2.5 oz / 70 g)
- 1 tablespoon olive oil (for greasing)
- 1 teaspoon garlic powder
- 1 teaspoon smoked paprika
- ½ teaspoon salt
- ¼ teaspoon black pepper
- Optional: Chopped parsley for garnish

Instructions:

1. **Preheat the Oven:** Preheat your oven to 425°F (220°C). Lightly grease a baking sheet with olive oil.
2. **Make the Honey Mustard Coating:** In a bowl, mix honey, Dijon mustard, garlic powder, smoked paprika, salt, and black pepper until well combined. Set aside a few tablespoons of the mixture for dipping.
3. **Coat the Chicken:** In a large bowl, toss the chicken pieces with the sourdough discard until coated. Dip each piece into the honey mustard mixture, then roll in sourdough breadcrumbs, pressing lightly to adhere.
4. **Bake the Chicken Bites:** Arrange the coated chicken bites on the prepared baking sheet. Bake for 20 minutes, flipping halfway through, until golden brown and crispy.
5. **Serve:** Garnish with chopped parsley and serve hot with the reserved honey mustard sauce for dipping.

Nutritional Values (per serving): Calories: 320 | Protein: 28g | Carbohydrates: 28g | Fat: 10g | Fiber: 1g | Sugar: 12g

MEDITERRANEAN SOURDOUGH FLATBREAD PIZZAS

Preparation Time: 15 minutes
Cooking Time: 15 minutes
Servings: Serves 4

The picture is only demonstrative of the recipe.

Ingredients:

- 1 cup sourdough discard (unfed)
- 1½ cups all-purpose flour (6.75 oz / 190 g)
- ½ cup warm water (4 oz / 120 ml)
- 2 tablespoons olive oil (1 oz / 30 ml) (plus extra for brushing)
- 1 teaspoon dried oregano
- ½ teaspoon salt
- ½ cup hummus (4 oz / 115 g) (for the base)
- 1 cup cherry tomatoes, halved (5 oz / 140 g)
- ½ cup crumbled feta cheese (2 oz / 60 g)
- ¼ cup sliced Kalamata olives (1 oz / 30 g)
- 1 tablespoon capers, drained (0.5 oz / 15 g)
- 1 teaspoon dried oregano (for topping)
- 1 cup fresh arugula (lightly packed, 1 oz / 30 g)
- Optional: Red pepper flakes for a spicy kick

Instructions:

1. **Make the Flatbread Dough:** In a large bowl, combine sourdough discard, warm water, olive oil, dried oregano, and salt. Gradually add flour, mixing until a soft, slightly sticky dough forms.
2. **Shape and Pre-Cook the Flatbreads:** Divide the dough into 4 equal portions. Roll each portion into a thin oval or round shape. Heat a large skillet or griddle over medium-high heat and brush with olive oil. Cook each flatbread for about 2 minutes per side until lightly golden but still soft.
3. **Assemble the Flatbreads:** Preheat your oven to 425°F (220°C). Place the pre-cooked flatbreads on a baking sheet. Spread a layer of hummus on each flatbread. Top with cherry tomatoes, crumbled feta, sliced Kalamata olives, and capers. Sprinkle with dried oregano.
4. **Bake:** Bake for about 8-10 minutes, or until the toppings are heated through and the flatbread edges are crispy.
5. **Garnish and Serve:** Remove from the oven and top with fresh arugula. Add red pepper flakes for extra heat if desired. Serve hot and enjoy the vibrant Mediterranean flavors.

Nutritional Values (per serving): Calories: 320 | Protein: 9g | Carbohydrates: 38g | Fat: 14g | Fiber: 4g | Sugar: 3g

ONE-PAN SOURDOUGH CHICKEN STIR FRY

Preparation Time: 15 minutes
Cooking Time: 20 minutes
Servings: Serves 4

The picture is only demonstrative of the recipe.

Ingredients:

- 1 cup sourdough discard (unfed)
- 1 lb (16 oz / 450 g) boneless, skinless chicken breast, cut into thin strips
- 2 tablespoons soy sauce (1 oz / 30 ml) (use tamari for gluten-free)
- 1 tablespoon honey (0.75 oz / 20 g)
- 1 tablespoon rice vinegar (0.5 oz / 15 ml)
- 1 tablespoon sesame oil (0.5 oz / 15 ml)
- 2 cloves garlic, minced
- 1 teaspoon grated fresh ginger
- 1 red bell pepper, thinly sliced (6 oz / 170 g)
- 1 cup broccoli florets (4 oz / 115 g)
- 1 cup snap peas (3 oz / 85 g)
- 2 green onions, chopped (1 oz / 30 g)
- 2 tablespoons sesame seeds (1 oz / 30 g) (for garnish)
- Optional: Red pepper flakes for heat

Instructions:

1. **Marinate the Chicken:** In a bowl, combine sourdough discard, soy sauce, honey, rice vinegar, garlic, and ginger. Add the chicken strips, tossing to coat. Let marinate for at least 10 minutes.
2. **Cook the Chicken:** Heat sesame oil in a large skillet or wok over medium-high heat. Add the marinated chicken (reserving the marinade) and cook for 5-7 minutes, stirring frequently, until browned and cooked through. Remove the chicken from the pan and set aside.
3. **Stir Fry the Vegetables:** In the same pan, add red bell pepper, broccoli florets, and snap peas. Stir fry for 4-5 minutes until tender-crisp.
4. **Combine and Finish:** Return the chicken to the pan along with the reserved marinade. Toss everything together and cook for another 2 minutes until heated through.
5. **Garnish and Serve:** Remove from heat and top with chopped green onions and sesame seeds. Add red pepper flakes if desired. Serve hot over rice or noodles.

Nutritional Values (per serving): Calories: 320 | Protein: 30g | Carbohydrates: 22g | Fat: 12g | Fiber: 4g | Sugar: 8g

SOURDOUGH BBQ PULLED PORK SLIDERS

Preparation Time: 15 minutes
Cooking Time: 6 hours (slow cooker) or 3 hours (oven)
Servings: Serves 4

The picture is only demonstrative of the recipe.

Ingredients:

For the Pulled Pork:

- 2 lbs (32 oz / 900 g) pork shoulder (boneless)
- 1 cup sourdough discard (unfed)
- 1 cup BBQ sauce (8 oz / 240 ml) (use your favorite brand)
- ½ cup apple cider vinegar (4 oz / 120 ml)
- 1 tablespoon smoked paprika
- 1 tablespoon garlic powder
- 1 teaspoon onion powder
- 1 teaspoon salt
- ½ teaspoon black pepper
- ½ teaspoon cayenne pepper (optional for extra heat)

For the Sliders:

- 8 mini sourdough slider buns
- 1 cup coleslaw (store-bought or homemade)
- ¼ cup sliced pickles (1 oz / 30 g)
- Optional: Extra BBQ sauce for drizzling

Instructions:

1. **Prepare the Pork:** In a bowl, mix smoked paprika, garlic powder, onion powder, salt, black pepper, and cayenne pepper. Rub this spice mixture all over the pork shoulder.
2. **Cook the Pork (Slow Cooker Method):** Place the seasoned pork in a slow cooker. Add sourdough discard, BBQ sauce, and apple cider vinegar. Cover and cook on low for 6-8 hours or on high for 4-5 hours, until the pork is tender and easily shredded. **(Oven Method):** Preheat the oven to 300°F (150°C). Place the pork in a roasting pan, cover tightly with foil, and bake for about 3 hours, basting occasionally with the cooking juices.
3. **Shred the Pork:** Once cooked, remove the pork from the slow cooker or oven and shred using two forks. Return the shredded pork to the sauce, stirring to coat evenly.

4. **Assemble the Sliders:** Slice the sourdough slider buns in half. Pile the pulled pork onto the bottom halves, top with coleslaw and sliced pickles, then cover with the top halves of the buns.
5. **Serve:** Serve warm with extra BBQ sauce for drizzling, if desired. Perfect for parties, game days, or a fun family meal.

Nutritional Values (per serving): Calories: 450 | Protein: 32g | Carbohydrates: 44g | Fat: 18g | Fiber: 3g | Sugar: 14g

SOURDOUGH CHICKEN QUESADILLAS

Preparation Time: 15 minutes
Cooking Time: 15 minutes
Servings: Serves 4

The picture is only demonstrative of the recipe.

Ingredients:

- 1 cup sourdough discard (unfed)
- 2 cups cooked chicken, shredded (10 oz / 280 g) (rotisserie chicken works well)
- 1 cup shredded Mexican cheese blend (4 oz / 115 g)
- ½ cup sourdough breadcrumbs (from stale sourdough bread, finely crushed)
- ¼ cup diced red onion (1.5 oz / 45 g)
- ¼ cup chopped cilantro (0.5 oz / 15 g)
- 1 jalapeño, seeded and finely chopped (optional for heat)
- 1 teaspoon smoked paprika
- 1 teaspoon garlic powder
- ½ teaspoon cumin
- ½ teaspoon salt
- 8 small flour tortillas
- 2 tablespoons olive oil (1 oz / 30 ml) (for frying)
- Optional: Sour cream, guacamole, or salsa for serving

Instructions:

1. **Make the Chicken Filling:** In a large bowl, combine shredded chicken, sourdough discard, diced red onion, chopped cilantro, jalapeño, smoked paprika, garlic powder, cumin, and salt. Mix until the chicken is evenly coated.
2. **Assemble the Quesadillas:** Lay out the tortillas. Sprinkle a layer of shredded Mexican cheese blend on half of each tortilla. Spoon the chicken mixture over the cheese, then sprinkle with sourdough breadcrumbs for extra crunch. Fold the tortillas in half to form semicircles.
3. **Cook the Quesadillas:** Heat olive oil in a large skillet over medium heat. Cook the quesadillas, two at a time, for about 3-4 minutes per side, or until golden brown and the cheese is melted.
4. **Serve:** Cut each quesadilla into wedges and serve hot with sour cream, guacamole, or salsa on the side. Perfect for a quick lunch, dinner, or party appetizer.

Nutritional Values (per serving): Calories: 390 | Protein: 22g | Carbohydrates: 30g | Fat: 20g | Fiber: 3g | Sugar: 3g

SOURDOUGH CRUST VEGGIE TART

Preparation Time: 20 minutes (plus 30 minutes chilling time)
Cooking Time: 30 minutes
Servings: Serves 4

The picture is only demonstrative of the recipe.

Ingredients:

For the Sourdough Crust:

- 1 cup sourdough discard (unfed)
- 1½ cups all-purpose flour (6.75 oz / 190 g)
- ½ cup cold unsalted butter, cubed (4 oz / 115 g)
- ½ teaspoon salt
- 2-3 tablespoons cold water (as needed)

For the Veggie Filling:

- 1 zucchini, thinly sliced (6 oz / 170 g)
- 1 red bell pepper, thinly sliced (6 oz / 170 g)
- ½ red onion, thinly sliced (2.5 oz / 70 g)
- 1 cup cherry tomatoes, halved (5 oz / 140 g)
- ½ cup crumbled goat cheese (2 oz / 60 g)
- 2 tablespoons olive oil (1 oz / 30 ml)
- 1 teaspoon dried oregano
- 1 teaspoon garlic powder
- ½ teaspoon salt
- ¼ teaspoon black pepper
- Optional: Fresh basil leaves for garnish

Instructions:

1. **Make the Sourdough Crust:** In a food processor, combine sourdough discard, flour, cold butter, and salt. Pulse until the mixture resembles coarse crumbs. Gradually add cold water, one tablespoon at a time, until the dough comes together. Form the dough into a ball, flatten into a disk, wrap in plastic wrap, and chill for at least 30 minutes.
2. **Preheat and Roll Out:** Preheat your oven to 400°F (200°C). On a floured surface, roll out the chilled dough into a 12-inch (30 cm) circle. Transfer to a parchment-lined baking sheet.

3. **Assemble the Tart:** Arrange the zucchini, red bell pepper, red onion, and cherry tomatoes on the crust, leaving a 1-inch (2.5 cm) border. Sprinkle with goat cheese, oregano, garlic powder, salt, and black pepper. Drizzle with olive oil. Fold the edges of the crust over the vegetables, pleating as needed.
4. **Bake the Tart:** Bake for 30 minutes, or until the crust is golden and the vegetables are tender.
5. **Garnish and Serve:** Let cool slightly before slicing. Garnish with fresh basil leaves if desired. Serve warm or at room temperature for a light lunch or dinner.

Nutritional Values (per serving): Calories: 350 | Protein: 9g | Carbohydrates: 36g | Fat: 19g | Fiber: 4g | Sugar: 6g

SOURDOUGH PIZZA CALZONES

Preparation Time: 20 minutes (plus 1 hour rising time)
Cooking Time: 25 minutes
Servings: Serves 4

The picture is only demonstrative of the recipe.

Ingredients:

For the Sourdough Dough:

- 1 cup sourdough discard (unfed)
- 2 cups all-purpose flour (9 oz / 255 g)
- ½ cup warm water (4 oz / 120 ml)
- 2 tablespoons olive oil (1 oz / 30 ml)
- 1 teaspoon salt
- 1 teaspoon dried Italian seasoning

For the Filling:

- 1 cup marinara sauce (8 oz / 240 ml) (plus extra for dipping)
- 1½ cups shredded mozzarella cheese (6 oz / 170 g)
- ½ cup sliced pepperoni (2 oz / 60 g)
- ½ cup sautéed mushrooms (3 oz / 85 g)
- ¼ cup chopped fresh basil (0.5 oz / 15 g)
- 1 teaspoon garlic powder
- 1 egg, beaten (for egg wash)
- Optional: Red pepper flakes for heat

Instructions:

1. **Make the Sourdough Dough:** In a large bowl, combine sourdough discard, warm water, olive oil, salt, and Italian seasoning. Gradually add flour, mixing until a soft, slightly sticky dough forms. Turn the dough onto a floured surface and knead for about 5 minutes until smooth and elastic. Place in a greased bowl, cover, and let rise in a warm place for 1 hour.
2. **Preheat and Divide:** Preheat your oven to 425°F (220°C). Line a baking sheet with parchment paper. Divide the risen dough into 4 equal portions and roll each into a circle about 8 inches (20 cm) in diameter.

3. **Fill the Calzones:** Spread a thin layer of marinara sauce on one half of each dough circle, leaving a border for sealing. Top with shredded mozzarella, pepperoni slices, sautéed mushrooms, and chopped basil. Sprinkle with garlic powder and red pepper flakes if desired.
4. **Seal and Brush:** Fold the other half of the dough over the filling to form a half-moon shape. Press the edges firmly with a fork to seal. Brush the tops with beaten egg for a golden finish.
5. **Bake:** Place the calzones on the prepared baking sheet and bake for 20-25 minutes, or until golden brown and crispy.
6. **Serve:** Allow to cool slightly before serving. Serve hot with extra marinara sauce on the side for dipping.

Nutritional Values (per serving): Calories: 420 | Protein: 18g | Carbohydrates: 48g | Fat: 18g | Fiber: 3g | Sugar: 6g

TANGY SOURDOUGH BEEF TACOS

Preparation Time: 15 minutes
Cooking Time: 20 minutes
Servings: Serves 4

The picture is only demonstrative of the recipe.

Ingredients:

- 1 cup sourdough discard (unfed)
- 1 lb (16 oz / 450 g) ground beef (85% lean)
- 1 small red onion, diced (4 oz / 115 g)
- 2 cloves garlic, minced
- 1 jalapeño, seeded and diced (optional for heat)
- 1 tablespoon chili powder
- 1 teaspoon cumin
- 1 teaspoon smoked paprika
- ½ teaspoon dried oregano
- ½ teaspoon salt
- ¼ teaspoon black pepper
- ½ cup sourdough breadcrumbs (from stale sourdough bread, finely crushed)
- 8 small corn tortillas
- 1 cup shredded lettuce (2 oz / 60 g)
- 1 cup diced tomatoes (5 oz / 140 g)
- ½ cup shredded cheddar cheese (2 oz / 60 g)
- ¼ cup sour cream (2 oz / 60 g)
- 2 tablespoons lime juice (1 oz / 30 ml)
- Optional: Fresh cilantro and lime wedges for garnish

Instructions:

1. **Cook the Ground Beef:** In a large skillet, cook the ground beef over medium-high heat until browned, breaking it up with a spatula as it cooks. Drain excess fat if necessary.
2. **Add the Seasonings:** Add diced red onion, minced garlic, and jalapeño (if using) to the skillet. Stir and cook until softened. Stir in chili powder, cumin, smoked paprika, oregano, salt, and black pepper.
3. **Incorporate the Sourdough:** Add sourdough discard and sourdough breadcrumbs to the skillet. Mix well to coat the beef evenly, letting the mixture cook for an additional 3-4 minutes until heated through.
4. **Warm the Tortillas:** In a dry skillet over medium heat, warm the corn tortillas for about 30 seconds per side until pliable.
5. **Assemble the Tacos:** Spoon the tangy sourdough beef mixture onto each tortilla. Top with shredded lettuce, diced tomatoes, shredded cheddar cheese, and a dollop of sour cream. Drizzle with lime juice for extra tang.
6. **Serve:** Garnish with fresh cilantro and lime wedges if desired. Serve hot and enjoy with your favorite salsa or guacamole.

Nutritional Values (per serving): Calories: 390 | Protein: 22g | Carbohydrates: 28g | Fat: 22g | Fiber: 4g | Sugar: 5g

BANANA CHIA SOURDOUGH MUFFINS

Preparation Time: 15 minutes
Cooking Time: 25 minutes
Servings: Serves 4

The picture is only demonstrative of the recipe.

Ingredients:

- 1 cup sourdough discard (unfed)
- 2 ripe bananas, mashed (about 1 cup / 8 oz / 225 g)
- ¼ cup honey (2 oz / 60 ml)
- ¼ cup coconut oil, melted (2 oz / 60 ml)
- 1 large egg
- 1 teaspoon vanilla extract
- 1 cup whole wheat flour (4.5 oz / 130 g)
- 2 tablespoons chia seeds (1 oz / 30 g)
- 1 teaspoon baking powder
- ½ teaspoon baking soda
- ½ teaspoon cinnamon
- ¼ teaspoon salt
- Optional: ¼ cup chopped walnuts (1 oz / 30 g) for topping

Instructions:

1. **Preheat the Oven:** Preheat your oven to 350°F (175°C). Line a muffin tin with paper liners or grease with coconut oil.
2. **Mix Wet Ingredients:** In a large bowl, combine sourdough discard, mashed bananas, honey, melted coconut oil, egg, and vanilla extract. Whisk until smooth and well combined.
3. **Combine Dry Ingredients:** In a separate bowl, mix whole wheat flour, chia seeds, baking powder, baking soda, cinnamon, and salt.
4. **Make the Batter:** Gradually fold the dry ingredients into the wet mixture until just combined. Do not overmix.
5. **Fill Muffin Tin:** Divide the batter evenly among the prepared muffin cups, filling each about three-quarters full. Sprinkle chopped walnuts on top, if desired.
6. **Bake:** Bake for 22-25 minutes, or until a toothpick inserted in the center of a muffin comes out clean.
7. **Cool and Serve:** Allow the muffins to cool in the tin for 5 minutes before transferring them to a wire rack to cool completely. Enjoy warm or at room temperature.

Nutritional Values (per serving): Calories: 250 | Protein: 5g | Carbohydrates: 35g | Fat: 10g | Fiber: 4g | Sugar: 14g

BLUEBERRY SOURDOUGH OAT BARS

Preparation Time: 15 minutes
Cooking Time: 30 minutes
Servings: Serves 4

The picture is only demonstrative of the recipe.

Ingredients:

- 1 cup sourdough discard (unfed)
- 1½ cups rolled oats (4.5 oz / 130 g)
- ½ cup whole wheat flour (2.25 oz / 65 g)
- ⅓ cup honey (3 oz / 85 g)
- ¼ cup coconut oil, melted (2 oz / 60 ml)
- 1 teaspoon vanilla extract
- ½ teaspoon cinnamon
- ¼ teaspoon salt
- 1½ cups fresh blueberries (9 oz / 255 g) (or frozen, thawed and drained)
- 1 tablespoon lemon juice (0.5 oz / 15 ml)
- 1 teaspoon cornstarch

Instructions:

1. **Preheat the Oven:** Preheat your oven to 350°F (175°C). Line an 8x8 inch (20x20 cm) baking pan with parchment paper, leaving an overhang for easy removal.
2. **Make the Oat Crust and Crumble:** In a large bowl, mix sourdough discard, rolled oats, whole wheat flour, honey, melted coconut oil, vanilla extract, cinnamon, and salt until well combined. The mixture should be slightly crumbly but stick together when pressed.
3. **Create the Blueberry Filling:** In a separate bowl, toss blueberries with lemon juice and cornstarch to coat evenly.
4. **Assemble the Bars:** Press about two-thirds of the oat mixture into the bottom of the prepared baking pan to form the crust. Spread the blueberry mixture evenly over the crust. Crumble the remaining oat mixture on top of the blueberries.
5. **Bake:** Bake for 30-35 minutes, or until the top is golden brown and the blueberries are bubbling.
6. **Cool and Serve:** Allow the bars to cool completely in the pan before lifting them out using the parchment overhang. Slice into squares and serve.

Nutritional Values (per serving): Calories: 280 | Protein: 5g | Carbohydrates: 45g | Fat: 10g | Fiber: 5g | Sugar: 20g

CHERRY ALMOND SOURDOUGH CRUMBLE

Preparation Time: 15 minutes
Cooking Time: 30 minutes
Servings: Serves 4

The picture is only demonstrative of the recipe.

Ingredients:

For the Cherry Filling:

- 3 cups pitted cherries (fresh or frozen, thawed and drained) (15 oz / 425 g)
- ¼ cup maple syrup (2 oz / 60 ml)
- 1 tablespoon lemon juice (0.5 oz / 15 ml)
- 1 tablespoon cornstarch

For the Almond Sourdough Crumble:

- 1 cup sourdough discard (unfed)
- 1 cup rolled oats (3 oz / 85 g)
- ½ cup almond flour (2 oz / 60 g)
- ¼ cup sliced almonds (1 oz / 30 g)
- ¼ cup coconut oil, melted (2 oz / 60 ml)
- ¼ cup coconut sugar (1.75 oz / 50 g)
- 1 teaspoon cinnamon
- ¼ teaspoon salt

Instructions:

1. **Preheat the Oven:** Preheat your oven to 350°F (175°C). Grease an 8x8 inch (20x20 cm) baking dish.
2. **Prepare the Cherry Filling:** In a bowl, mix pitted cherries, maple syrup, lemon juice, and cornstarch until the cherries are evenly coated. Spread the cherry mixture evenly in the prepared baking dish.
3. **Make the Almond Sourdough Crumble:** In another bowl, combine sourdough discard, rolled oats, almond flour, sliced almonds, melted coconut oil, coconut sugar, cinnamon, and salt. Mix until crumbly and well combined.
4. **Top and Bake:** Sprinkle the almond sourdough crumble evenly over the cherry filling. Bake for 30-35 minutes, or until the topping is golden brown and the cherries are bubbly.
5. **Cool and Serve:** Allow the crumble to cool for at least 10 minutes before serving. Enjoy warm or at room temperature, optionally with a scoop of vanilla yogurt or ice cream.

Nutritional Values (per serving): Calories: 310 | Protein: 6g | Carbohydrates: 42g | Fat: 14g | Fiber: 6g | Sugar: 22g

COCONUT LIME SOURDOUGH COOKIES

Preparation Time: 15 minutes
Cooking Time: 12 minutes
Servings: Serves 4

The picture is only demonstrative of the recipe.

Ingredients:

- 1 cup sourdough discard (unfed)
- ½ cup unsweetened shredded coconut (2 oz / 60 g)
- ½ cup coconut oil, melted (4 oz / 115 g)
- ⅓ cup coconut sugar (2.5 oz / 70 g)
- 1 large egg
- Zest of 2 limes (about 2 tablespoons)
- 1 tablespoon lime juice (0.5 oz / 15 ml)
- 1½ cups all-purpose flour (6.75 oz / 190 g)
- ½ teaspoon baking powder
- ¼ teaspoon baking soda
- ¼ teaspoon salt
- Optional: Extra lime zest for garnish

Instructions:

1. **Preheat the Oven:** Preheat your oven to 350°F (175°C). Line a baking sheet with parchment paper.
2. **Mix Wet Ingredients:** In a large bowl, combine sourdough discard, melted coconut oil, coconut sugar, egg, lime zest, and lime juice. Whisk until smooth and well combined.
3. **Combine Dry Ingredients:** In a separate bowl, mix all-purpose flour, shredded coconut, baking powder, baking soda, and salt.
4. **Make the Dough:** Gradually add the dry ingredients to the wet mixture, stirring until just combined. Do not overmix.
5. **Shape the Cookies:** Using a tablespoon, scoop the dough and roll into balls. Place them on the prepared baking sheet about 2 inches apart. Press each ball lightly with your palm to flatten.
6. **Bake:** Bake for 10-12 minutes, or until the edges are lightly golden.
7. **Cool and Serve:** Allow the cookies to cool on the baking sheet for 5 minutes before transferring them to a wire rack to cool completely. Garnish with extra lime zest if desired.

Nutritional Values (per serving): Calories: 250 | Protein: 3g | Carbohydrates: 31g | Fat: 13g | Fiber: 2g | Sugar: 15g

DARK CHOCOLATE SOURDOUGH BARK

Preparation Time: 15 minutes (plus 30 minutes chilling time)
Cooking Time: 5 minutes
Servings: Serves 4

The picture is only demonstrative of the recipe.

Ingredients:

- 1 cup sourdough discard (unfed)
- 8 oz (225 g) dark chocolate (70% cocoa or higher), chopped
- ½ cup sourdough breadcrumbs (from stale sourdough bread, finely crushed)
- ¼ cup chopped nuts (e.g., almonds, walnuts, or pistachios) (1 oz / 30 g)
- ¼ cup dried cranberries (1.5 oz / 45 g)
- 1 tablespoon coconut oil (0.5 oz / 15 ml)
- 1 teaspoon vanilla extract
- ¼ teaspoon sea salt (for sprinkling)
- Optional: 1 tablespoon cacao nibs (0.5 oz / 15 g) for extra crunch

Instructions:

1. **Prepare the Baking Sheet:** Line a baking sheet with parchment paper.
2. **Melt the Chocolate:** In a microwave-safe bowl, combine dark chocolate and coconut oil. Microwave in 30-second intervals, stirring between each, until fully melted and smooth. Alternatively, melt the chocolate in a heatproof bowl over a pot of simmering water (double boiler method).
3. **Combine Ingredients:** Stir in sourdough discard and vanilla extract until well combined. Fold in sourdough breadcrumbs for extra crunch.
4. **Spread the Chocolate Mixture:** Pour the chocolate mixture onto the prepared baking sheet, spreading it into a thin layer (about ¼ inch thick).
5. **Add Toppings:** Sprinkle chopped nuts, dried cranberries, and cacao nibs (if using) evenly over the chocolate layer. Finish with a light sprinkle of sea salt.
6. **Chill and Break into Pieces:** Place the baking sheet in the refrigerator for at least 30 minutes, or until the chocolate is fully set. Once firm, break the chocolate bark into irregular pieces.
7. **Serve and Store:** Serve immediately or store in an airtight container in the refrigerator for up to 2 weeks.

Nutritional Values (per serving): Calories: 250 | Protein: 4g | Carbohydrates: 30g | Fat: 15g | Fiber: 5g | Sugar: 16g

FIG AND WALNUT SOURDOUGH ENERGY SQUARES

Preparation Time: 15 minutes (plus 1 hour chilling time)
Cooking Time: No baking required
Servings: Serves 4

The picture is only demonstrative of the recipe.

Ingredients:

- 1 cup sourdough discard (unfed)
- 1 cup dried figs, chopped (5 oz / 140 g)
- ½ cup rolled oats (1.5 oz / 45 g)
- ½ cup walnuts, chopped (2 oz / 60 g)
- ¼ cup almond butter (2 oz / 60 g)
- ¼ cup honey (2 oz / 60 ml)
- 1 teaspoon vanilla extract
- ½ teaspoon cinnamon
- ¼ teaspoon salt
- Optional: 1 tablespoon chia seeds (0.5 oz / 15 g) for extra fiber

Instructions:

1. **Prepare the Baking Dish:** Line an 8x8 inch (20x20 cm) baking dish with parchment paper, leaving an overhang for easy removal.
2. **Mix Wet Ingredients:** In a large bowl, combine sourdough discard, almond butter, honey, and vanilla extract. Stir until smooth and well combined.
3. **Add Dry Ingredients:** Fold in chopped figs, rolled oats, chopped walnuts, cinnamon, salt, and chia seeds (if using). Mix until evenly distributed. The mixture should be thick and sticky.
4. **Press into Pan:** Transfer the mixture into the prepared baking dish. Use a spatula to press it down firmly and evenly.
5. **Chill and Set:** Refrigerate for at least 1 hour, or until firm.
6. **Cut into Squares:** Once set, lift the mixture out using the parchment overhang. Cut into squares or bars of desired size.
7. **Serve and Store:** Serve immediately or store in an airtight container in the refrigerator for up to 1 week. Perfect for on-the-go snacking or a quick energy boost.

Nutritional Values (per serving): Calories: 280 | Protein: 6g | Carbohydrates: 38g | Fat: 12g | Fiber: 5g | Sugar: 22g

GINGERBREAD SOURDOUGH LOAF

Preparation Time: 15 minutes
Cooking Time: 45 minutes
Servings: Serves 4

The picture is only demonstrative of the recipe.

Ingredients:

- 1 cup sourdough discard (unfed)
- 1½ cups all-purpose flour (6.75 oz / 190 g)
- ½ cup molasses (6 oz / 170 g)
- ¼ cup coconut oil, melted (2 oz / 60 ml)
- ¼ cup coconut sugar (1.75 oz / 50 g)
- 1 large egg
- 1 teaspoon vanilla extract
- 1 tablespoon ground ginger
- 1 teaspoon cinnamon
- ½ teaspoon ground cloves
- ½ teaspoon baking soda
- ½ teaspoon salt
- ¼ cup chopped crystallized ginger (1.5 oz / 45 g) (optional for extra zing)
- Optional: Powdered sugar for dusting

Instructions:

1. **Preheat the Oven:** Preheat your oven to 350°F (175°C). Grease a 9x5 inch (23x13 cm) loaf pan or line it with parchment paper.
2. **Mix Wet Ingredients:** In a large bowl, combine sourdough discard, molasses, melted coconut oil, coconut sugar, egg, and vanilla extract. Whisk until smooth and well combined.
3. **Combine Dry Ingredients:** In a separate bowl, mix all-purpose flour, ground ginger, cinnamon, ground cloves, baking soda, and salt.
4. **Make the Batter:** Gradually add the dry ingredients to the wet mixture, stirring until just combined. Fold in chopped crystallized ginger for an extra burst of flavor, if desired.
5. **Pour and Smooth:** Pour the batter into the prepared loaf pan, spreading it evenly with a spatula.
6. **Bake:** Bake for 40-45 minutes, or until a toothpick inserted in the center comes out clean.
7. **Cool and Serve:** Allow the loaf to cool in the pan for 10 minutes before transferring it to a wire rack to cool completely. Dust with powdered sugar for a festive touch, if desired.

Nutritional Values (per serving): Calories: 300 | Protein: 5g | Carbohydrates: 50g | Fat: 9g | Fiber: 2g | Sugar: 25g

GREEK YOGURT SOURDOUGH PARFAITS

Preparation Time: 15 minutes
Cooking Time: None (No-bake recipe)
Servings: Serves 4

The picture is only demonstrative of the recipe.

Ingredients:

- 1 cup sourdough discard (unfed)
- 2 cups Greek yogurt (16 oz / 450 g) (plain or vanilla)
- ½ cup sourdough granola (from stale sourdough bread, finely crumbled)
- ½ cup mixed berries (blueberries, raspberries, strawberries) (3 oz / 85 g)
- 2 tablespoons honey (1 oz / 30 ml)
- 1 teaspoon vanilla extract
- ¼ teaspoon cinnamon
- Optional: 2 tablespoons chopped nuts (e.g., almonds, walnuts) (1 oz / 30 g) for extra crunch

Instructions:

1. **Prepare the Yogurt Base:** In a bowl, mix Greek yogurt, sourdough discard, honey, vanilla extract, and cinnamon until smooth and well combined.
2. **Layer the Parfaits:** In 4 serving glasses, layer the parfaits as follows:
   - Start with a spoonful of the yogurt mixture at the bottom.
   - Add a layer of mixed berries.
   - Sprinkle a layer of sourdough granola.
   - Repeat the layers until the glasses are filled, ending with a topping of berries and a drizzle of honey.
3. **Add Crunch (Optional):** Sprinkle chopped nuts on top for extra crunch and texture, if desired.
4. **Chill and Serve:** Serve immediately or refrigerate for up to 2 hours to allow the flavors to meld. Enjoy cold as a healthy breakfast, snack, or dessert.

Nutritional Values (per serving): Calories: 220 | Protein: 12g | Carbohydrates: 28g | Fat: 8g | Fiber: 3g | Sugar: 18g

HONEY SOURDOUGH APPLE CRISP

Preparation Time: 15 minutes
Cooking Time: 35 minutes
Servings: Serves 4

The picture is only demonstrative of the recipe.

Ingredients:

For the Apple Filling:

- 4 medium apples, peeled, cored, and sliced (about 1.5 lbs / 680 g) (Honeycrisp or Granny Smith work well)
- ¼ cup honey (2 oz / 60 ml)
- 1 tablespoon lemon juice (0.5 oz / 15 ml)
- 1 teaspoon cinnamon
- ¼ teaspoon nutmeg
- 1 tablespoon cornstarch

For the Sourdough Crisp Topping:

- 1 cup sourdough discard (unfed)
- ¾ cup rolled oats (2.25 oz / 65 g)
- ½ cup almond flour (2 oz / 60 g)
- ¼ cup chopped pecans (1 oz / 30 g)
- ¼ cup coconut oil, melted (2 oz / 60 ml)
- ¼ cup honey (2 oz / 60 ml)
- 1 teaspoon vanilla extract
- ½ teaspoon cinnamon
- ¼ teaspoon salt

Instructions:

1. **Preheat the Oven:** Preheat your oven to 350°F (175°C). Grease an 8x8 inch (20x20 cm) baking dish.
2. **Prepare the Apple Filling:** In a bowl, combine sliced apples, honey, lemon juice, cinnamon, nutmeg, and cornstarch. Toss until the apples are evenly coated. Spread the apple mixture evenly in the prepared baking dish.
3. **Make the Sourdough Crisp Topping:** In a separate bowl, mix sourdough discard, rolled oats, almond flour, chopped pecans, melted coconut oil, honey, vanilla extract, cinnamon, and salt until well combined and crumbly.
4. **Assemble and Bake:** Sprinkle the sourdough crisp topping evenly over the apple mixture. Bake for 30-35 minutes, or until the topping is golden brown and the apples are tender and bubbling.
5. **Cool and Serve:** Allow the crisp to cool for at least 10 minutes before serving. Serve warm, optionally with a dollop of Greek yogurt or a scoop of vanilla ice cream.

Nutritional Values (per serving): Calories: 320 | Protein: 5g | Carbohydrates: 52g | Fat: 12g | Fiber: 6g | Sugar: 34g

LEMON POPPY SEED SOURDOUGH CAKE

Preparation Time: 20 minutes
Cooking Time: 35 minutes
Servings: Serves 4

The picture is only demonstrative of the recipe.

Ingredients:

For the Cake:

- 1 cup sourdough discard (unfed)
- 1 cup all-purpose flour (4.5 oz / 130 g)
- ½ cup almond flour (2 oz / 60 g)
- ½ cup coconut sugar (3.5 oz / 100 g)
- ⅓ cup melted coconut oil (2.5 oz / 75 ml)
- ¼ cup lemon juice (2 oz / 60 ml)
- Zest of 2 lemons (about 2 tablespoons)
- 2 large eggs
- 2 tablespoons poppy seeds (1 oz / 30 g)
- 1 teaspoon baking powder
- ½ teaspoon baking soda
- ½ teaspoon vanilla extract
- ¼ teaspoon salt

For the Lemon Glaze (Optional):

- ½ cup powdered sugar (2 oz / 60 g)
- 2 tablespoons lemon juice (1 oz / 30 ml)

Instructions:

1. **Preheat the Oven:** Preheat your oven to 350°F (175°C). Grease a 9x5 inch (23x13 cm) loaf pan or line it with parchment paper.
2. **Mix Wet Ingredients:** In a large bowl, whisk together sourdough discard, melted coconut oil, lemon juice, lemon zest, eggs, and vanilla extract until smooth.
3. **Combine Dry Ingredients:** In a separate bowl, mix all-purpose flour, almond flour, coconut sugar, poppy seeds, baking powder, baking soda, and salt.

4. **Make the Batter:** Gradually add the dry ingredients to the wet mixture, stirring until just combined. Do not overmix.
5. **Pour and Smooth:** Pour the batter into the prepared loaf pan, spreading it evenly with a spatula.
6. **Bake:** Bake for 30-35 minutes, or until a toothpick inserted in the center comes out clean.
7. **Cool and Glaze (Optional):** Allow the cake to cool in the pan for 10 minutes before transferring it to a wire rack to cool completely. For the glaze, whisk together powdered sugar and lemon juice until smooth. Drizzle over the cooled cake.
8. **Serve:** Slice and serve as a light, refreshing dessert or snack.

Nutritional Values (per serving): Calories: 320 | Protein: 6g | Carbohydrates: 42g | Fat: 15g | Fiber: 3g | Sugar: 20g

MAPLE PECAN SOURDOUGH CLUSTERS

Preparation Time: 10 minutes
Cooking Time: 20 minutes
Servings: Serves 4

The picture is only demonstrative of the recipe.

Ingredients:

- 1 cup sourdough discard (unfed)
- 1½ cups pecan halves (6 oz / 170 g)
- ¼ cup rolled oats (0.75 oz / 20 g)
- ¼ cup pure maple syrup (2 oz / 60 ml)
- 2 tablespoons coconut oil, melted (1 oz / 30 ml)
- 1 teaspoon vanilla extract
- ½ teaspoon cinnamon
- ¼ teaspoon salt
- Optional: 1 tablespoon chia seeds (0.5 oz / 15 g) for extra crunch

Instructions:

1. **Preheat the Oven:** Preheat your oven to 325°F (165°C). Line a baking sheet with parchment paper.
2. **Combine Wet Ingredients:** In a large bowl, mix sourdough discard, maple syrup, melted coconut oil, and vanilla extract until smooth.
3. **Mix in Dry Ingredients:** Fold in pecan halves, rolled oats, cinnamon, salt, and chia seeds (if using). Stir until the pecans and oats are well coated with the sourdough mixture.
4. **Form Clusters:** Using a spoon, drop clusters of the mixture onto the prepared baking sheet, leaving space between each for even baking.
5. **Bake:** Bake for 18-20 minutes, or until golden brown and fragrant. Rotate the baking sheet halfway through for even cooking.
6. **Cool and Set:** Allow the clusters to cool completely on the baking sheet, where they will harden as they cool.
7. **Serve and Store:** Enjoy immediately or store in an airtight container at room temperature for up to a week. Perfect for snacking, breakfast toppings, or gifting.

Nutritional Values (per serving): Calories: 280 | Protein: 4g | Carbohydrates: 22g | Fat: 22g | F iber: 4g | Sugar: 12g

PEACH SOURDOUGH COBBLER

Preparation Time: 15 minutes
Cooking Time: 35 minutes
Servings: Serves 4

The picture is only demonstrative of the recipe.

Ingredients:

For the Peach Filling:

- 4 cups sliced ripe peaches (fresh or frozen, thawed and drained) (20 oz / 570 g)
- ¼ cup honey (2 oz / 60 ml)
- 1 tablespoon lemon juice (0.5 oz / 15 ml)
- 1 tablespoon cornstarch
- 1 teaspoon vanilla extract
- ½ teaspoon cinnamon

For the Sourdough Topping:

- 1 cup sourdough discard (unfed)
- 1 cup all-purpose flour (4.5 oz / 130 g)
- ¼ cup coconut sugar (1.75 oz / 50 g)
- 1 teaspoon baking powder
- ½ teaspoon baking soda
- ½ teaspoon cinnamon
- ¼ teaspoon salt
- ¼ cup coconut oil,melted (2oz / 60 ml)
- ¼ cup almond milk (2 oz / 60 ml) (or any milk of choice)

Instructions:

1. **Preheat the Oven:** Preheat your oven to 350°F (175°C). Grease an 8x8 inch (20x20 cm) baking dish.
2. **Prepare the Peach Filling:** In a bowl, mix sliced peaches, honey, lemon juice, cornstarch, vanilla extract, and cinnamon. Toss until the peaches are well coated. Spread the peach mixture evenly in the prepared baking dish.
3. **Make the Sourdough Topping:** In a separate bowl, combine sourdough discard, all-purpose flour, coconut sugar, baking powder, baking soda, cinnamon, and salt. Stir in melted coconut oil and almond milk until just combined. The batter should be thick but spreadable.
4. **Top the Peaches:** Drop spoonfuls of the sourdough topping over the peach filling, spreading it gently to cover most of the fruit. It's okay if some of the peaches peek through.
5. **Bake:** Bake for 30-35 minutes, or until the topping is golden brown and the peaches are bubbly.
6. **Cool and Serve:** Allow the cobbler to cool for at least 10 minutes before serving. Serve warm, optionally with a scoop of vanilla ice cream or a dollop of Greek yogurt.

Nutritional Values (per serving): Calories: 320 | Protein: 5g | Carbohydrates: 52g | Fat: 10g | Fiber: 4g | Sugar: 30g

PUMPKIN SPICE SOURDOUGH DONUTS

Preparation Time: 15 minutes
Cooking Time: 15 minutes
Servings: Serves 4

The picture is only demonstrative of the recipe.

Ingredients:

For the Donuts:

- 1 cup sourdough discard (unfed)
- 1 cup pumpkin puree (8 oz / 225 g)
- ½ cup coconut sugar (3.5 oz / 100 g)
- ¼ cup coconut oil, melted (2 oz / 60 ml)
- 2 large eggs
- 1 teaspoon vanilla extract
- 1½ cups all-purpose flour (6.75 oz / 190 g)
- 1 teaspoon baking powder
- ½ teaspoon baking soda
- 1½ teaspoons pumpkin pie spice
- ½ teaspoon cinnamon
- ¼ teaspoon salt

For the Cinnamon Sugar Coating:

- ¼ cup coconut sugar (1.75 oz / 50 g)
- 1 teaspoon cinnamon
- 2 tablespoons melted coconut oil (1 oz / 30 ml) for brushing

Instructions:

1. **Preheat the Oven:** Preheat your oven to 350°F (175°C). Grease a donut pan with coconut oil or non-stick spray.
2. **Mix Wet Ingredients:** In a large bowl, combine sourdough discard, pumpkin puree, coconut sugar, melted coconut oil, eggs, and vanilla extract. Whisk until smooth and well combined.
3. **Combine Dry Ingredients:** In a separate bowl, mix all-purpose flour, baking powder, baking soda, pumpkin pie spice, cinnamon, and salt.

4. **Make the Batter:** Gradually add the dry ingredients to the wet mixture, stirring until just combined. Do not overmix.
5. **Fill the Donut Pan:** Spoon the batter into the prepared donut pan, filling each cavity about three-quarters full. Smooth the tops with a spatula.
6. **Bake:** Bake for 12-15 minutes, or until a toothpick inserted in the center comes out clean.
7. **Cool and Coat:** Allow the donuts to cool in the pan for 5 minutes before transferring them to a wire rack. Brush each donut with melted coconut oil and dip in the cinnamon sugar mixture to coat.
8. **Serve:** Serve warm or at room temperature. Enjoy with a hot cup of coffee or tea for the perfect autumn treat.

Nutritional Values (per serving): Calories: 280 | Protein: 5g | Carbohydrates: 38g | Fat: 12g | Fiber: 3g | Sugar: 18g

CHAPTER 5: ADVANCED TECHNIQUES – ELEVATE YOUR SOURDOUGH GAME

Experimenting with Different Flours for Unique Flavors

The choice of flour significantly impacts the flavor, texture, and fermentation process of sourdough. While all-purpose and bread flour provide consistency, experimenting with alternative flours can enhance complexity and depth.

- **Whole Wheat Flour** – Adds a nutty, earthy flavor and increases fermentation activity due to higher nutrient content. Best used in combination with white flour to maintain elasticity.
- **Rye Flour** – Produces a dense, moist crumb with deep, tangy notes. It's lower in gluten, so it benefits from blending with higher-protein flours.
- **Spelt Flour** – Slightly sweet with a mild nuttiness. It absorbs water differently, making dough more delicate. Handle gently to avoid over-fermentation.
- **Einkorn Flour** – One of the oldest grains, providing a rich, buttery taste. It's lower in gluten, so it requires shorter fermentation times.
- **Kamut Flour** – Enhances the dough with a golden hue and a slightly sweet flavor, adding depth to sourdough loaves.
- **Alternative Grains (Buckwheat, Barley, Oats, Cornmeal, etc.)** – Often used in smaller percentages to introduce unique flavors and textures.

Tips for Success:

- Adjust hydration levels since different flours absorb water at different rates.
- Start with a small percentage (10-30%) of alternative flours and gradually increase.
- Be mindful of fermentation times—whole grains and ancient grains ferment faster.

By experimenting with flour combinations, you can craft sourdough loaves with distinct textures and flavors tailored to your preference.

How to Achieve Beautiful Scoring Designs Without Special Tools

Scoring is essential for controlling oven spring and creating artistic designs on your sourdough. While a professional bread lame (razor tool) provides precision, you can achieve excellent results with simple tools and techniques.

Alternative Scoring Tools:

- **Sharp Kitchen Knife** – Works well for bold, rustic cuts. Use a long, serrated knife for best results.
- **Scissors** – Ideal for creating dramatic ear-like flaps in the crust. Snip the surface at an angle.
- **Razor Blade (Unattached)** – If you don't have a lame, a single-edge razor blade can be held carefully for detailed designs.

- **Bench Scraper** – Can be pressed lightly into the dough for geometric patterns.

Techniques for Better Scoring:

1. **Chill the Dough** – Refrigerated dough is firmer, making clean cuts easier.
2. **Dust with Flour** – A light dusting of flour before scoring highlights the design post-bake.
3. **Hold at an Angle** – A 30-45° blade angle creates an ear (a crisp, lifted crust edge).
4. **Make Confident Cuts** – Use swift, decisive motions to prevent dragging the dough.
5. **Adjust Depth** – Deeper cuts (¼-½ inch) allow for more dramatic expansion, while shallow cuts create delicate surface patterns.

Practice Ideas:

- **Classic Ear** – One long curved slash along the side of the dough.
- **Leaf or Wheat Pattern** – Several diagonal slashes along a central line.
- **Crosshatch** – A crisscross pattern, great for boules.
- **Minimalist Slashes** – One or two clean, straight cuts for a modern look.

Even without professional tools, thoughtful scoring can add a personal touch and elevate the aesthetics of your sourdough bread.

Creating Flavored Sourdough – Herbs, Cheese, Chocolate, and More

Flavored sourdough is an excellent way to personalize your bread. Whether savory or sweet, incorporating additional ingredients enhances aroma, texture, and taste.

Savory Add-Ins:

- **Herbs & Spices** – Rosemary, thyme, garlic, cumin, fennel, or smoked paprika add depth.
- **Cheese** – Cheddar, parmesan, gouda, or blue cheese provide richness.
- **Olives & Sun-Dried Tomatoes** – Bring a Mediterranean flair and umami notes.
- **Caramelized Onions & Roasted Garlic** – Enhance sweetness and complexity.

Sweet Add-Ins:

- **Chocolate & Cocoa** – Dark chocolate chunks or cocoa powder create a rich, indulgent loaf.
- **Dried Fruits & Nuts** – Cranberries, raisins, figs, walnuts, or pecans add chew and crunch.
- **Cinnamon & Spices** – Perfect for breakfast-style sourdough with a warm, spiced aroma.
- **Citrus Zest & Honey** – Brightens flavor and adds a delicate sweetness.

How to Incorporate Add-Ins Successfully:

1. **Choose the Right Stage** – Mix-ins should be folded in during the last stretch-and-fold phase to prevent gluten disruption.
2. **Avoid Excess Moisture** – Drain wet ingredients like olives or fruit to avoid overhydration.
3. **Balance Flavor Intensity** – A small amount (10-20% of total flour weight) goes a long way.
4. **Distribute Evenly** – Fold ingredients gently to ensure they're well distributed.

Experimenting with flavors allows for endless possibilities, making each loaf a unique culinary experience.

Gluten-Free and Vegan Sourdough – How to Make It Work

Making gluten-free or vegan sourdough requires adjustments to maintain structure and fermentation activity.

Gluten-Free Sourdough:

Since traditional sourdough relies on gluten for elasticity and rise, gluten-free loaves require a combination of alternative flours and binders.

Flour Options:

- **Brown Rice Flour** – Provides a mild, slightly sweet flavor.
- **Sorghum Flour** – Adds protein and a light texture.
- **Buckwheat Flour** – Imparts an earthy taste with a denser crumb.
- **Tapioca & Potato Starch** – Help improve chewiness and softness.

Essential Binders:

- **Psyllium Husk** – Mimics gluten by providing elasticity.
- **Ground Flaxseeds or Chia Seeds** – Work as natural thickeners.

- **Xanthan Gum or Guar Gum** – Improve texture and help retain moisture.

Baking Adjustments:

- Increase **hydration** (gluten-free flours absorb more water).
- Extend **fermentation time** (wild yeast takes longer to rise in gluten-free dough).
- Use a **pan or mold** to support structure since gluten-free dough is softer.

Vegan Sourdough:

Most traditional sourdough recipes are naturally vegan, but some enriched versions (such as brioche) include dairy or eggs.

Common Vegan Substitutes:

- **Butter → Coconut Oil or Vegan Butter**
- **Milk → Almond, Oat, or Soy Milk**
- **Eggs (for enrichment) → Flax Egg (1 Tbsp flaxseed + 3 Tbsp water)**

Maintaining Flavor and Fermentation Activity:

- Use **apple cider vinegar or citrus juice** to enhance tanginess.
- Maintain a **well-fed starter**, as gluten-free flours ferment differently than wheat.
- Add **pre-soaked seeds** (like sunflower or pumpkin) for extra texture.

Creating gluten-free and vegan sourdough requires adjustments, but with the right techniques, you can achieve delicious, satisfying loaves.

Final Thoughts

Mastering advanced sourdough techniques opens up a world of creativity and customization. Whether experimenting with different flours, perfecting scoring designs, infusing bold flavors, or crafting gluten-free and vegan variations, each step refines your skills and deepens your understanding of fermentation.

The beauty of sourdough lies in its adaptability—by applying these techniques, you'll elevate your baking, producing exceptional loaves that reflect your unique style.

CHAPTER 6: TROUBLESHOOTING & SOURDOUGH FAQS

Solve Any Baking Problem!

Even the most experienced sourdough bakers encounter challenges. Whether your loaf refuses to rise, tastes too sour (or not sour enough), or turns out too dense, don't worry—every problem has a solution. This guide helps you diagnose and fix common sourdough issues, ensuring consistent, bakery-quality results every time.

WHY ISN'T MY BREAD RISING?

A disappointing rise usually results from weak starter activity, fermentation issues, or improper dough handling. Here's how to fix it.

1. Weak or Inactive Starter

Your sourdough starter is the engine behind your bread's rise. If it's sluggish, your dough won't have the strength to expand.

- **Check for Activity:** A healthy starter should double or triple in volume within 4–6 hours after feeding, with a bubbly, slightly tangy aroma.
- **Feed Consistently:** Use a 1:1:1 ratio (equal parts starter, flour, and water by weight). In colder environments, feed twice daily and keep it in a warm spot (75–82°F / 24–28°C).
- **Use Whole Grain Flour:** Rye or whole wheat flour provides extra nutrients for fermentation, strengthening the starter.

2. Under-Fermentation

If fermentation is cut short, the dough lacks gas production and elasticity, resulting in a dense, flat loaf.

- **Extend Bulk Fermentation:** Most sourdough needs 4–6 hours at room temperature (75°F / 24°C). If your kitchen is cooler, it may take longer.

- **Perform the Poke Test:** Gently press the dough with a floured finger. If it springs back slowly and leaves a slight indentation, it's ready.

3. Over-Fermentation or Over-Proofing

Over-fermented dough loses structure and collapses.

- **Shorten Proofing Time:** If your dough spreads too much before baking, reduce the final proof. Cold-proofing for 8–12 hours instead of overnight can help.
- **Reshape Before Baking:** If over-proofed, gently reshape to rebuild surface tension.

4. Incorrect Flour or Hydration

- **Use Strong Flour:** Bread flour (12–14% protein) provides better gluten structure than all-purpose flour.
- **Adjust Hydration:** Too much water makes dough slack and prevents proper rise. Start with 70% hydration and adjust based on your flour type.

WHY DOES MY BREAD TASTE TOO SOUR / NOT SOUR ENOUGH?

Sourdough flavor is shaped by fermentation, temperature, hydration, and starter maintenance.

If Your Bread Is Too Sour

- **Reduce Cold Fermentation:** Long cold-proofing (24–48 hours) encourages acetic acid production, making the bread sharper and more vinegary. Try reducing cold-proof time to 8–12 hours or proofing at room temperature instead.
- **Feed Starter More Frequently:** An underfed starter develops too much acidity. Feed at least twice daily at warm room temperature (75–82°F / 24–28°C).
- **Increase Hydration:** More water (75–80%) encourages lactic acid production, which creates a milder tang.

If Your Bread Lacks Flavor

- **Extend Bulk Fermentation:** Short fermentation leads to bland bread. Allow at least 4–6 hours at room temperature.
- **Use a Mature Starter:** A young starter (less than a week old) lacks enough developed acidity to provide a complex sourdough flavor.
- **Lower Hydration Slightly:** Drier dough (65–70% hydration) can intensify flavor by concentrating fermentation byproducts.
- **WHY IS MY STARTER NOT BUBBLY?**

If your starter isn't rising or bubbling, it might need a boost.

1. Inconsistent Feeding Schedule

- **Stick to Regular Feedings:** A neglected starter may turn sluggish. Feed every 12–24 hours at room temperature using a 1:2:2 ratio (starter:flour:water).
- **Use Filtered or Dechlorinated Water:** Chlorine in tap water can slow fermentation.

2. Temperature Issues

- **Keep It Warm:** Starters thrive between 75–82°F (24–28°C). If your kitchen is cold, place it in a proofing box, near a warm appliance, or in the oven with the light on.

3. Wrong Flour Choice

- **Switch to Whole Wheat or Rye:** These flours provide extra nutrients and encourage more active fermentation.

4. Over-Acidification

- **Refresh with More Flour:** If your starter smells like vinegar or acetone, it's too acidic. Feed it with a higher flour ratio (1:3:3) and refresh more frequently.

WHY IS MY BREAD TOO DENSE?

A dense loaf is usually caused by under-fermentation, weak gluten development, or poor shaping.

1. Under-Fermentation

If the dough hasn't built enough gas, it will be heavy and tight-crumbed.

- **Extend Bulk Fermentation:** Aim for 4–6 hours at room temperature (or longer in cooler environments).
- **Check Your Starter:** Ensure it's doubling in size within 4–6 hours after feeding.

2. Weak Gluten Development

Strong gluten traps gas for a light, open crumb.

- **Use Bread Flour:** Flour with 12–14% protein provides better gluten structure.
- **Incorporate Stretch and Folds:** Perform 3–4 sets during the first 2 hours of bulk fermentation to strengthen gluten without over-kneading.
- **Try an Autolyse:** Let flour and water rest for 30–60 minutes before adding starter and salt to improve gluten formation.

3. Over- or Under-Proofing

- **Perform the Poke Test:** Under-proofed dough feels dense and springs back immediately. Over-proofed dough feels weak and collapses when touched.

4. Baking Issues

- **Preheat the Oven Well:** Bake at 475°F (246°C) with a baking stone or Dutch oven for the best oven spring.
- **Use Steam:** Steam keeps the crust soft during the first 20 minutes, allowing maximum rise. Bake with a covered Dutch oven or place a tray of hot water in the oven.

FINAL TROUBLESHOOTING CHECKLIST

- **Starter is doubling in size within 4–6 hours of feeding?** If not, refresh with whole wheat flour and feed consistently.
- **Dough is properly fermented?** Extend bulk fermentation if dough lacks volume.
- **Shaping builds enough tension?** Dough should feel taut and smooth before proofing.
- **Oven is preheated properly?** Bake at 475°F (246°C) with steam for the best results.

Mastering sourdough takes patience, but every challenge is an opportunity to learn. By making small adjustments, you'll achieve beautifully risen, flavorful loaves every time. Keep practicing, take notes, and enjoy the process!

Quick Reference Troubleshooting Chart

This quick reference troubleshooting chart is designed to help you swiftly identify and resolve common sourdough baking issues. Whether your bread isn't rising, the crust is too hard, or the crumb is too dense, this guide will lead you to the solution. Keep this chart handy as your go-to resource for diagnosing problems and perfecting every loaf.

1. Dough Not Rising Properly

Issue	Possible Cause	Solution
Dough is flat and dense	Weak or inactive starter	Refresh starter with 1:2:2 feeding ratio, ensuring it doubles in size before use. Keep starter at 75-82°F (24-28°C).
	Under-fermentation	Extend bulk fermentation time. Use the poke test to check readiness.

Issue	Possible Cause	Solution
	Cool room temperature	Ferment in a warmer spot (75-82°F / 24-28°C) or use a proofing box.
Dough rises but then collapses	Over-proofing	Shorten proofing time. Perform the poke test: if the dent doesn't spring back, it's over-proofed.
	Weak gluten structure	Use bread flour with at least 12% protein. Perform stretch and folds to strengthen gluten.
	Insufficient surface tension	Tighten shaping technique. Ensure the dough is taut and smooth before final proof.

2. Dense or Gummy Crumb

Issue	Possible Cause	Solution
Tight, dense crumb	Under-fermentation	Allow longer bulk fermentation at room temperature (4-6 hours at 75°F / 24°C).
	Insufficient hydration	Increase hydration to 70-85% based on flour type and environmental humidity.
	Weak gluten development	Perform stretch and folds during bulk fermentation for strength.
	Low-protein flour	Use high-protein bread flour (12-14% protein content) for better structure.
Gummy or sticky crumb	Over-hydration	Reduce hydration by 5-10%. Dough should be tacky, not overly sticky.
	Under-baking	Extend baking time by 10-15 minutes. Ensure internal temperature is at least 200°F (93°C).

3. Flat or Misshapen Loaf

Issue	Possible Cause	Solution
Loaf spreads sideways	Weak surface tension	Improve shaping technique for a tighter, more elastic outer layer.
	Over-proofing	Reduce final proofing time. Perform the poke test for accuracy.
	Insufficient flour strength	Use higher protein flour or blend with whole grain for added structure.

Issue	Possible Cause	Solution
Loaf bursts unevenly during baking	Improper scoring	Score at a 30° angle with a sharp blade to control expansion.
	Insufficient surface tension	Tighten shaping technique to prevent bursting.

4. Crust Issues

Issue	Possible Cause	Solution
Crust is too hard	Insufficient steam	Bake in a Dutch oven or use a steam tray for the first 20 minutes.
	Over-baking	Reduce baking time or lower oven temperature by 25°F (14°C).
Crust is too soft	Insufficient browning time	Remove the lid or steam tray after 20 minutes for dry heat exposure.
	Low oven temperature	Preheat to at least 475°F (246°C) for optimal oven spring.
Pale crust	Insufficient sugar (Maillard reaction)	Add a small amount of honey or malt powder to the dough.
	Low baking temperature	Increase oven temperature for better caramelization.

5. Flavor Issues

Issue	Possible Cause	Solution
Bread is too sour	Long, cold fermentation	Shorten cold proofing time to 8-12 hours or proof at room temperature.
	Overly mature starter	Feed starter more frequently or at a 1:2:2 ratio for balanced acidity.
	Low hydration	Increase hydration to promote lactic acid (milder flavor) over acetic acid.
Bread is too bland	Short fermentation time	Extend bulk fermentation and/or proofing time for deeper flavor.
	Weak starter activity	Ensure starter is fully active and doubling before using in dough.
	High hydration	Reduce hydration slightly for a more concentrated flavor.

6. Sourdough Starter Problems

Issue	Possible Cause	Solution
Starter not bubbly or active	Infrequent feeding	Feed every 12-24 hours at room temperature. Use a 1:2:2 ratio for better activity.
	Low ambient temperature	Place in a warmer spot (75-82°F / 24-28°C) or use warm water for feeding.
	Poor water quality	Use filtered or dechlorinated water to avoid inhibiting yeast growth.
Starter smells like vinegar or acetone	Over-acidification	Discard most of the starter and refresh with a 1:3:3 feeding ratio.
	Infrequent feeding	Increase feeding frequency to reduce acidity and balance yeast activity.

7. Common Techniques and Tips

Problem Area	Quick Tip
Weak oven spring	Ensure high initial oven temperature (475°F / 246°C). Use steam for the first 20 minutes.
Uneven crumb structure	Perform consistent stretch and folds. Maintain consistent dough temperature during bulk fermentation.
Scoring difficulties	Use a sharp blade at a 30° angle. Score confidently and swiftly.
Flat, dense loaf	Check starter activity before mixing. Ensure adequate bulk fermentation time.

Final Tips for Consistent Success

- **Maintain a Baking Journal:** Document each bake, including flour type, hydration, fermentation time, temperature, and results. This helps you understand how each variable affects the outcome.
- **Experiment and Adjust:** Sourdough is influenced by environmental factors. Don't hesitate to adjust hydration, fermentation time, or temperature to achieve your desired results.
- **Patience and Practice:** Mastering sourdough requires patience and practice. Learn from each bake and keep refining your techniques.

Mastering Troubleshooting with Confidence

This quick reference chart empowers you to identify and solve common sourdough baking issues with precision and confidence. By understanding the variables involved and making informed adjustments, you'll consistently produce beautiful, flavorful loaves with an airy crumb and perfect crust. Whether you're a beginner or an experienced baker, this guide is your key to mastering the art of sourdough baking.

Made in United States
Cleveland, OH
29 June 2025

18104160R00046